新时代行业英语系列教材

总主编 姜　宏　　　　编　者 冯茂芳

主　编 刘　莉　　　　原版作者 Ernesto D'Acunto

副主编 刘　玥　王鸣爽

运输与物流英语
ENGLISH for
Transport & Logistics

清华大学出版社
北京

北京市版权局著作权合同登记号　图字：01-2021-1545

图书在版编目（CIP）数据

运输与物流英语 / 姜宏总主编；刘莉主编. —北京：清华大学出版社，2021.4
新时代行业英语系列教材
ISBN 978-7-302-57797-3

Ⅰ.①运…　Ⅱ.①姜…　②刘…　Ⅲ.①交通运输–英语–高等职业教育–教材②物流–英语–高等职业教育–教材
Ⅳ.①U②F25

中国版本图书馆 CIP 数据核字（2021）第 055426 号

策划编辑：刘细珍
责任编辑：刘细珍
封面设计：子　一
责任校对：王凤芝
责任印制：丛怀宇

出版发行：清华大学出版社
　　　　　网　　址：http://www.tup.com.cn，http://www.wqbook.com
　　　　　地　　址：北京清华大学学研大厦 A 座　　邮　编：100084
　　　　　社 总 机：010-62770175　　　　　　邮　购：010-62786544
　　　　　投稿与读者服务：010-62776969，c-service@tup.tsinghua.edu.cn
　　　　　质 量 反 馈：010-62772015，zhiliang@tup.tsinghua.edu.cn
印 装 者：北京博海升彩色印刷有限公司
经　　销：全国新华书店
开　　本：210mm×285mm　　**印　张**：7.5　　　**字　数**：180 千字
版　　次：2021 年 4 月第 1 版　　　　**印　次**：2021 年 4 月第 1 次印刷
定　　价：49.00 元

产品编号：091252-01

在经济全球化和国际交往日益频繁的今天，无论是作为个人还是组织的一员，参与国际交流与合作都需要具备良好的外语沟通能力和扎实的专业技术能力。高职院校承担着培养具有全球竞争力的高端技术人才的使命，需要探索如何有效地培养学生的行业外语能力。行业外语教学一直是职业院校的短板，缺少合适的教材是其中一个主要原因。目前，国内大多数高职院校在第一学年开设公共英语课程，所用教材多为通用英语教材，其主题与学生所学专业的关联度总体较低；部分院校自主开发的行业英语教材，在专业内容的系统性、语言表达的准确性等方面存在诸多不足；还有部分院校直接采用国外原版的大学本科或研究生教材，但这些教材学术性和专业性太强，对以就业为导向的高职院校学生来说，十分晦涩难懂。

清华大学出版社从欧洲引进原版素材并组织国内一线行业英语教师改编的这套"新时代行业英语系列教材"，以提升学生职业英语能力为目标，服务师生教与学。本套教材具有如下特点：

一、编写理念突出全球化和国际化

本套教材在欧洲原版引进优质资源的基础上改编而成，全球化视角选材，结合行业领域和单元主题，关注环境保护、人口老龄化、贫困等时代难题，培养学生的国际视野和世界公民素养。单元主题、板块编排和练习设计与国际接轨，体现国际规范和国际标准，且反映全球行业发展动态和前景，帮助学生全面了解全球行业现状和掌握国际操作流程，夯实行业知识体系。

二、编写目标注重培养学生使用英语完成工作任务的实际应用能力

为响应高职院校外语教学改革号召，培养具有国际竞争力的高端技术人才，将外语教学目标由原来的语言能力导向转变为职业能力导向，本套教材通过听、说、读、写、译等基本语言技能训练，让学生完成不同行业领域的工作任务，将英语放到职场的背景中来学，放到员工的岗位职责、工作流程中来学。

三、结构与内容紧扣行业领域的职场情境和核心业务

本套教材围绕行业核心概念和业务组织教学单元，不同单元相互关联，内容由浅入深、由易到难，循序渐进；教材各单元主题契合行业典型工作场景，内容反映职业岗位核心业务知识与流程。每本教材根据内容设置 8 至 10 个单元，用多种形式的语言训练任务提升学生对行业知识的理解与应用。

四、资源立体多样，方便师生教与学

本套教材图文并茂。通过改编，在原版教材基础上每个单元增加了学习目标，明确了学生在完成各单元学习后应该达到的知识和能力水平；增加了重点词汇中文注释和专业术语表，便于学生准确理解行业核心概念；听力练习和阅读篇章均配有音频，并借助二维码扫码听音的形式呈现，实现教材的立体化，方便学生学习；习题安排契合单元的主题内容，便于检测单元学习目标的实现程度。教材另配有电子课件和习题答案，方便教师备课与授课。教师可以征订教材后联系出版社索取。

本套教材共10本，包括《护理英语》《机电英语》《建筑工程英语》《运输与物流英语》《烹饪、餐饮与接待英语》《旅游英语》《银行与金融英语》《市场营销与广告英语》《商务英语》《商务会谈英语》，涵盖医药卫生、机电设备、土木建筑、交通运输、旅游、财经商贸等六大类专业。建议高职院校结合本校人才培养目标，开设相应课程。

本套教材适合作为高职院校学生的行业英语教材，也适合相关行业从业人员作为培训或自学教材。

姜宏

2021年3月31日

专门用途英语（ESP）目标明确，针对性和实用性强，与高职院校培养高素质技术技能人才的目标相适应，受到高职教育工作者的关注和重视，ESP课程教学在许多高职院校也得到了有益的尝试与探索。但高质量的ESP英语教学一定是建立在使用适应学习者学习需求、反映行业规范和发展动态的优秀教材基础之上的。

《运输与物流英语》在清华大学出版社引进的 *Flash on English for Transport and Logistics* 基础上改编而成，反映了国际货运代理和物流行业的最新发展和国际规范，适合经济全球化背景下国际物流、国际商务和国际贸易类学生提高专业外语水平使用。

本教材共分为10个单元，包括：运输方式、驾驶舱、定位工具、气象与运输、多式联运货物运输、货物装卸、运输单据、运输保险、安全法规、工作申请等运输与物流相关内容。

本教材具有以下特点：

1.针对性强——面向国际化交通运输与物流管理类专业学生与专业技术人员

本教材基于国际货运代理和物流行业选取典型工作情境和工作内容，以专业人才高质量就业和专业发展为目标，教材内容反映最新的行业发展和行业规范，不仅适用于高职高专相关专业的学生，也适用于物流、国际货运代理和国际贸易及相关从业者。

2.实用性强——融英语语言能力训练和职业领域工作能力培养为一体

本教材重视学生英语语言能力的训练，每单元均列出词汇表，学习任务分为导学、听、说、读、写和专业术语六个板块；同时，语言训练任务比较充分地展示了物流行业的职场环境和工作任务，为学习者提升工作环境下的职业英语能力创设条件。

3.可读性强——教材语料地道，图文并茂，引人入胜

本教材教学资料均来自英语国家的原始语言材料，语境真实，语言地道，精美的配图很容易引发学习者的学习兴趣，提高学习效率。

向本套教材的总主编姜宏教授表示感谢！由于编者水平有限，书中错漏之处在所难免，敬请专家、读者批评指正。

编者

2021年1月

Contents

Learning Objectives

Upon completion of the unit, students will be able to:

- identify different forms of transport;
- master the words and expressions related to transport;
- compare the advantages and disadvantages of different forms of transport;
- cultivate the awareness of environmental protection when choosing from different means of transport.

Starting Off

1 **Write each means of transport under the picture.**

articulated lorry	barge	cargo plane	container ship	goods train	ferry
lorry	road tanker	road train	tanker	van	

1) _____

2) _____

3) _____

4) _____

5) _____

6) _____

7) _____

8) _____

9) _____

10) _____

11) _____

MY GLOSSARY

articulated lorry	铰链式卡车
barge	*n.* 驳船, 平底载货船
cargo plane	运输飞机, 货运飞机
container ship	集装箱运货船
goods train	货运列车, 运货列车
ferry	*n.* 渡船, 渡轮
lorry	*n.* 卡车, 货车
road tanker	公路运油车; 缸车
road train	道路列车; 重型汽车列车
tanker	*n.* 油船; 槽车
van	*n.* 厢形货车, 有盖小货车

Transport by land

Road transport or **road haulage** is the most common form of land transport. Over short and medium distances it is **relatively** fast and **convenient**, which makes it **particularly suitable** for **perishable goods** such as fresh food **produce**. Goods can be **loaded** and **unloaded** at any **destination** so it is **extremely flexible**. However, **due to** the limited carrying **capacity**, it is not so **economical** for long distances.

A company can use its own transport services, such as vans for local **deliveries**, or can use the services of a **courier** or a road haulage firm which can **deliver** goods both nationally and internationally. A TIR lorry (from the French Transports Internationaux Routiers) is **normally** used when transporting goods across multiple **borders**. The goods are loaded into containers which are **sealed** at their point of **departure** and therefore do not need to be inspected by **customs** officials until the final destination.

ADVANTAGES
- door-to-door delivery
- fairly fast
- relatively cost-effective

DISADVANTAGES
- air pollution and environmental damage
- limited capacity/weight
- delays due to **congested** roads, bad weather

Although the use of rail as a method of transport has **declined** in favour of road transport, it is a very efficient and **cost-effective** way of transporting heavy and bulky goods over long distances. It is less flexible than road transport, operating to fixed time schedules, and goods need to be **transferred** at both ends of the journey. Container trains have solved this problem for some goods since containers can easily be loaded to ships or lorries to continue on to their destination.

ADVANTAGES
- low-cost and **environmental impact**
- low-accident rate
- suitable for large quantities and long distances

DISADVANTAGES
- slow
- limited by the rail network coverage
- size limits (due to bridges and tunnels)

road haulage		公路货运
relatively	adv.	相当地; 相对地
convenient	adj.	方便的, 便利的
particularly	adv.	特别, 尤其
suitable	adj.	适宜的, 合适的
perishable goods		易腐烂商品, 易变质商品
produce	n.	食品; 农产品
load	v.	装, 装载
unload	v.	卸(货)
destination	n.	目的地, 终点
extremely	adv.	非常, 极其; 极端
flexible	adj.	可变动的, 灵活的, 可变通的
due to		由于, 因为
capacity	n.	容积, 容量; 生产能力
economical	adj.	经济的, 省钱的; 节约的

delivery	n.	运送, 递送, 投递
courier	n.	信使, 递送员
deliver	v.	运送, 递送, 投递
normally	adv.	通常, 平常, 一般地
border	n.	国境; 边界, 边境
seal	v.	封, 密封
departure	n.	离开, 启程, 出发
customs	n.	海关
decline	v.	降低, 减少; 衰落
cost-effective	adj.	有成本效益的; 物有所值的, 合算的
transfer	v.	搬, 转移
congest	v.	(使)挤满, (使)拥堵
environmental	adj.	环境的, 周围的; 有关环境的
impact	n./v.	影响, 作用

2 Read the texts and answer the questions.

1) Which factors can influence the choice of transport?

2) Which is the most common form of transport by land?

3) Why is road transport flexible?

4) What is a TIR lorry and when and how is it used?

5) Which is the most suitable form of land transport for long distances? Why?

6) What is a container train?

7) What are the advantages and disadvantages of rail?

8) What is the major disadvantage of road transport impacting on the environment?

3 Match each word with the correct definition.

1)	convenient	a	☐ giving good value for money
2)	economical	b	☐ right or appropriate for a particular person, purpose, or situation
3)	suitable	c	☐ effective or productive in relation to its cost
4)	flexible	d	☐ restricted in size, amount, or extent
5)	cost-effective	e	☐ situated to allow easy access
6)	limited	f	☐ able to be easily modified to respond to altered circumstances

Reading 2

Transport by water

Transporting goods by **canal** or river is a cheap form of transport, but it is slow. Britain has a large network of canals, built during **the Industrial Revolution** to link the north and south of the country, but road and rail transport have taken over as they are much faster. There are 37,000 km of **inland waterways** in Europe, such as **the Rhine** and **the Danube**, which connect major cities and industrial areas, so there is **significant potential** to increase the share of **freight** transported by inland waterways within Europe.

Sea freight refers to the movement of goods by ship across seas and oceans and it is the most widely used form of transport for international trade. It can be divided into two types:

- **coastal shipping**, which is between the main ports within the same country;
- **overseas** shipping, which is between ports in different countries.

Overseas shipping is an economical means to transport a wide range of goods, from raw materials to plant machinery and vehicles since **virtually** no weight or size restrictions apply. Goods are normally packed in containers which means they can be loaded and unloaded onto the ship quickly and cheaply. The **merchandise** is well protected during transport, which reduces damage and the risk of loss or theft.

ADVANTAGES
- not congested, low-environmental impact

DISADVANTAGES
- slow, not fully **integrated** as part of **intermodal** transport

ADVANTAGES
- cheap
- suitable for long distances
- capable of carrying large **volumes**

DISADVANTAGES
- slow
- affected by bad weather
- huge environmental impact in case of accident

MY GLOSSARY

canal	n.	运河; 渠
the Industrial Revolution		工业革命
inland	adj.	内陆的, 内地的
waterway	n.	航道; 水路
the Rhine		莱茵河
the Danube		多瑙河
significant	adj.	重要的; 显著的
potential	n.	潜力, 潜能
freight	n.	货物; 货运

coastal	adj.	海岸的; 临海的, 沿海的
shipping	n.	运输;（尤指）船运, 海运
overseas	adj. /adv.	在海外（的）; 从国外来（的）; 到国外（的）
virtually	adv.	事实上, 几乎; 实质上
merchandise	n.	商品; 货物
integrated	adj.	综合的; 集成的
intermodal	adj.	联合的; 联运的
volume	n.	量; 体积

4 Read the texts and decide if these sentences are true (*T*) or false (*F*). Correct the false ones.

	T	F
1) In the UK, canal transport was used during the Industrial Revolution.	☐	☐
2) Canal transport is still a popular form of transport today.	☐	☐
3) Inland waterways in Europe are used to their full potential.	☐	☐
4) Transport by water is generally cheaper but slower than other forms.	☐	☐
5) Sea freight is the most common form of transport for international trade.	☐	☐
6) Only lightweight goods can be transported by sea.	☐	☐
7) Containers help reduce risks during transport.	☐	☐
8) Intermodal transport is where there are multiple destinations for cargo.	☐	☐

Reading 3

Container ports

Modern **ports** cover vast areas of water and land and handle hundreds of thousands of **tonnes** of cargo every year. Made of steel, containers are of a standard size, normally 20 foot or 40 foot long. When transporting goods it is possible to have a Full Container Load (FCL) where the container holds only the goods of a single customer. In this case, the container is usually loaded and sealed at **origin** and then opened at its final destination. The other possibility is a Less than Container Load (LCL), when the goods of more than one customer are grouped together into a container.

Two methods used for unloading and loading operations are:

- Lift-On Lift-Off (often abbreviated to Lo/Lo). The loading and unloading of ships is carried out by **cranes** and **derricks** which can lift the cargo, often containers, on and off the ship.
- Roll-on Roll-off (often abbreviated to Ro/Ro). This system is used on ships which have a **ramp**, so that vans, lorries or railroad cars with their cargo can be driven on and off the ship. It is also used for cars on **passenger** ferries.

MY GLOSSARY

port	n. 港市, 港口
tonne	n. 吨
origin	n. 出发地; 起源, 源头; 起因
crane	n. 起重机, 吊车

derrick	n. （港口装卸货物的）长臂吊车, 长臂起重机
ramp	n. （人造）斜坡, 坡道
passenger	n. 乘客, 旅客

5 Read the text and complete these sentences.

1) _____ make freight transportation easier.

2) Containers are of a standard size although _____ exist.

3) If a customer has enough goods to fill one container, it is called a _____.

4) With a FCL, a container is not normally _____ between its origin and destination.

5) If several customers have goods in a container, it is called a _____.

6) Ro/Ro and Lo/Lo are two examples of _____.

Reading 4

Transport by air

Air freight is the fastest **mode** of transport. It has always been used for high value **commodities**, **fragile**, perishable and urgently needed goods since it can **guarantee** such a quick delivery. The commercial life of perishable goods is short, so it is really only air freight that can guarantee moving the goods from **producer** to **consumer** in a **sufficiently** short time for the product to be sold. The costs **involved** are high, but this can be **justified** if the final consumers pay a **premium**. Similarly for other goods, the advantages of quick, safe air freight and savings **in terms of packing** and **insurance**, can **offset** the higher transportation costs. For these reasons, there has been an increase in the number of **airlines** operating cargo **aircraft** in recent years.

ADVANTAGES
- fast
- quick **administrative** process
- safe and secure

DISADVANTAGES
- expensive
- risk of delays caused by bad weather and strikes
- only suitable for small, lightweight goods

mode	*n.*	方法, 做法, 方式
commodity	*n.*	商品, 货物
fragile	*adj.*	易损坏的, 易碎的; 脆弱的
guarantee	*v.*	保证, 担保, 保障
producer	*n.*	生产者, 生产公司, 出产国
consumer	*n.*	消费者, 顾客, 用户
sufficiently	*adv.*	充足地, 足够地
involve	*v.*	包括, 包含
justify	*v.*	证明……正当(或有理、正确), 是……的正当理由
premium	*n.*	加价, 附加费; 津贴, 奖金
in terms of		在……方面, 从……方面来说; 根据……来看
packing	*n.*	包装; 包装材料; 行李
insurance	*n.*	保险
offset	*v.*	抵消, 补偿, 弥补
airline	*n.*	航空公司
aircraft	*n.*	飞机; 飞行器, 航空器
administrative	*adj.*	管理的

6 Read the text and answer the questions.

1) What kind of goods are often transported by air?

2) Why is air transport particularly suitable for perishable goods?

3) Is the final price that consumers pay affected by this choice of transport? How?

4) In what ways can using air transport save other costs?

5) How can bad weather affect air transport?

6) What are the major advantages of air freight?

Reading 5

The environmental impact of freight traffic

The total volume of **freight transport** around the world has a **massive** impact on the environment. Leaving aside environmental **disasters**, such as **spills** of **toxic waste** or **leaks** in **oil pipelines**, each mode of transport pollutes our air and water **to a** lesser or greater **extent**.

Aviation

Aviation is one of the fastest growing sources of **greenhouse gas emissions**. It also creates noise pollution, particularly damaging in **residential areas** located near major airports. The reductions in GHG (Greenhouse gases) have not been sufficient to **compensate** for the rapid growth of global air traffic, both passenger and cargo. Passengers, in fact, have to offset the emissions by paying a **surcharge**.

Road transport

Heavy goods vehicles are responsible for more harmful pollution than any other form of transport. They **emit particulates**, that is **microscopic specks of soot** and other matter invisible to the naked eye, which may cause **asthma**, lung cancer and **cardiovascular** issues. Vehicles also contribute to the increase of greenhouse gas emissions, as well as noise pollution. To reduce emissions and also to save money, smart **logistics** and GPS Systems can be used to ensure that vehicles use the best **routes** for multiple deliveries, avoiding "empty" return journeys.

Rail transport

This is the most **environmentally-friendly** form of transport. Studies show that it is between three and ten times less CO_2 **intensive** than road or air transport. The most negative impact comes from the **construction** of new lines and the **maintenance** of the existing network, as well as from accidents like leaks and spills of dangerous goods.

Sea transport

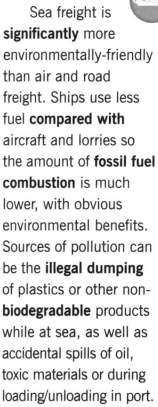

Sea freight is **significantly** more environmentally-friendly than air and road freight. Ships use less fuel **compared with** aircraft and lorries so the amount of **fossil fuel combustion** is much lower, with obvious environmental benefits. Sources of pollution can be the **illegal dumping** of plastics or other non-**biodegradable** products while at sea, as well as accidental spills of oil, toxic materials or during loading/unloading in port.

MY GLOSSARY

freight transport		货物运输
massive	*adj.*	巨大的; 大量的
disaster	*n.*	灾难, 灾祸; 不幸
spill	*n.*	溢出; 漏损
toxic waste		有毒废物, 毒废料
leak	*n.*	泄漏; 漏洞
oil pipeline		输油管道
to a...extent		到……程度, 到……地步
aviation	*n.*	航空; 飞行术
greenhouse gas emission		温室气体排放
residential area		住宅区, 居民区
compensate	*v.*	补偿, 赔偿
surcharge	*n.*	额外费用, 附加费
emit	*v.*	散发; 发出, 射出
particulate	*n.*	微粒
microscopic specks of soot		微小的烟灰斑点

asthma	*n.*	哮喘, 气喘
cardiovascular	*adj.*	心血管的
logistics	*n.*	物流; 后勤
route	*n.*	路线, 航线
environmentally-friendly	*adj.*	环保的, 对环境无害的
intensive	*adj.*	密集的, 集中的
construction	*n.*	建造, 构筑, 建设
maintenance	*n.*	维护, 维修
significantly	*adv.*	非常, 大大地
compared with		与……相比
fossil fuel		矿物燃料
combustion	*n.*	燃烧; 氧化; 骚动
illegal	*adj.*	非法的, 违法的
dumping	*n.*	倾倒, 丢弃, 抛弃
biodegradable	*adj.*	能进行生物降解的

7 Read the text and write which form(s) of transport these sentences refer to.

1) responsible for greenhouse gas emissions _____

2) causes disasters and severe damage _____

3) creates noise pollution _____

4) the best form of transport for the environment _____

5) illegal practices can harm the environment _____

6) improved technology can help reduce negative effects _____

7) causes the emission of particulates _____

8) uses less fuel compared with aircraft _____

Speaking

8 In pairs, analyse the information in the table and answer the questions.

World's Largest Container Ports

1989		2014	
Name of Port	**Volume, million TEUs***	**Name of Port**	**Volume, million TEUs**
Hong Kong (China)	4.5	Shanghai (China)	35.29
Singapore	4.4	Singapore	33.87
Rotterdam (Netherlands)	3.9	Shenzhen (China)	24.04
Kaohsiung (Taiwan, China)	3.4	Hong Kong (China)	22.23
Kobe (Japan)	2.5	Ningbo-Zhoushan (China)	19.45
Busan (South Korea)	2.2	Busan (South Korea)	18.68
Los Angeles (United States)	2.1	Qingdao (China)	16.62
New York / New Jersey (United States)	2.0	Guangzhou Harbor (China)	16.63
Keelung (Taiwan, China)	1.8	Jebel Ali, Dubai (United Arab Emirates)	15.25
Hamburg (Germany)	1.8	Los Angeles / Long Beach (USA)	15.16

Source: Containerisation International

TEU* stands for "Twenty-foot Equivalent Unit". This is the industry standard to measure containers and refers to the standard 20 foot container (20 ft long x 8 ft wide or 6.09 metres x 2.4 metres).

1) What information does the table give?

2) What years are compared?

3) In what unit of measurement is the data presented?

4) Which port was the biggest in 1989? What position did it hold in 2014?

5) Which port was the biggest in 2014? And what position did it hold in 1989?

6) What can you notice about the position of European ports in the period between 1989 and 2014?

7) Which continent had the most ports on the list in 2014?

8) What do you think these changes show?

9 **In pairs, decide the best method of transport for each of these situations. Consider all the forms of transport presented in this unit and give your reasons.**

1) books from an e-commerce website to its international, private customers

2) vans from a manufacturing plant in the north of England to a showroom in the south of the country

3) crude oil from Egypt to Europe

4) bananas from Brazil to a wholesaler in the USA

5) large, antique furniture from a wholesaler in India to a retailer in the UK

6) components from Detroit, USA, to an industrial plant in the south of Germany

7) leather goods from a manufacturer in Florence to a selection of retailers in the north of Italy

Technical Terms

Full Container Load (FCL)   集装箱整箱货物

Less than Container Load (LCL)   拼箱货

Lift-On Lift-Off (Lo/Lo)   吊上吊下船

Roll-on Roll-off (Ro/Ro)   滚装船

GHG (Greenhouse gases)   温室效应气体

GPS (Global Positioning System)   全球定位系统

TEU   全称Twenty-feet Equivalent Unit, 又称20英尺集装箱的换算单位, 也是国际标准箱的通用单位; 通常TEU被用来表示船舶能够装载集装箱的能力, 也可以用于统计集装箱和港口的吞吐量

Learning Objectives

Upon completion of the unit, students will be able to:

- identify the control space of different forms of transport;
- master the words and expressions related to control space of transport;
- distinguish the functions of the control space of different forms of transport.

1 **Match the following names with the pictures. Then read the text and check your answers.**

1) cab   **2)** cockpit   **3)** bridge   **4)** cabin

Each form of transport has its own particular area from where the driver controls the vehicle's movements. In a car the driver sits at the wheel for example. But the names we give to this area change from one form of transport to the other. The captain of a ship controls the vessel from the bridge, a lorry driver in a cabin, a pilot in a cockpit or flight deck, and a train driver in a cab.

Reading 1

The cockpit

A **cockpit** or **flight deck** is the area, usually near the front of an aircraft, from which a **pilot** controls the aircraft. Most modern cockpits are **enclosed**, except on some small aircraft, and cockpits on large airliners are also **physically** separated from the cabin. An aircraft is controlled both on the ground and in the air from the cockpit.

As a term for the pilot's **compartment** in an aircraft the term "cockpit" first appeared in 1914. After 1935 cockpit was also used informally to refer to the driver's seat of a car, especially a high **performance** one, and this is official **terminology** in Formula One. The term is probably related to the sailing term for the **coxswain**'s station in a Royal Navy ship, and later the location of the ship's **rudder** controls.

The cockpit of an aircraft contains flight instruments on an instrument panel, and the controls which enable the pilot to fly the aircraft. In most airliners, a door separates the cockpit from the passenger compartment. After the terrorist attacks of 11 September 2001, all major airlines **fortified** the cockpit against access by **hijackers**.

cockpit	*n.*	（飞机的）驾驶舱；（赛车的）驾驶座
flight deck		（飞机的）驾驶舱
pilot	*n.*	飞行员, 领航员
enclosed	*adj.*	封闭的
physically	*adv.*	物理上地; 身体上地
compartment	*n.*	隔间
performance	*n.*	性能, 效能; 表现
terminology	*n.*	术语
coxswain	*n.*	舵手; 艇长
rudder	*n.*	船舵;飞机方向舵
fortify	*v.*	加强, 增强
hijacker	*n.*	劫机者, 强盗

2 Read the text and answer the questions.

1) Where are cockpits usually located on aircraft?

2) When was the term "cockpit" first used for aviation?

3) What does the term usually refer to on a road?

4) What does it refer to on a ship?

5) What type of instruments does the cockpit of an aircraft contain?

6) Why is it separated by a door from the passenger compartment?

3 Match these words with their definitions.

1) cockpit   a ☐ an airplane used for carrying passengers

2) pilot   b ☐ the place where instruments are mounted on

3) airliner   c ☐ the enclosed space in an aircraft for the crew and passengers

4) cabin   d ☐ the space in an airplane which contains the flying controls

5) panel   e ☐ the person who operates an aircraft in flight

4 Look at these words. Find their synonyms from the text.

1) space   _____

2) airplane   _____

3) land   _____

4) section   _____

5) command   _____

5 Provide at least one question for each of the paragraphs describing the common flight instruments. The first one is done for you.

 Altimeter. The altimeter shows the aircraft's altitude above sea-level. A pressure altimeter, or barometric altimeter, is used by pilots to measure their elevation.
What does the altimeter show?
What is its function?

 Airspeed indicator. The airspeed indicator shows the aircraft's speed (usually in knots) relative to the surrounding air. The indicated airspeed must be corrected for air density (which varies with altitude, temperature and humidity) in order to obtain the true airspeed, and for wind conditions in order to obtain the speed over the ground.
1) _____ ?
2) _____ ?

 Vertical speed indicator. The VSI senses changing air pressure, and displays that information to the pilot as a rate of climb or descent in feet per minute, metres per second or knots.
1) _____
_____ ?
2) _____
_____ ?

 Attitude indicator. The attitude indicator (also known as an artificial horizon) shows the aircraft's attitude relative to the horizon. From this instrument the pilot can see if the wings are level and if the aircraft's nose is pointing above or below the horizon. This primary instrument is also useful in conditions of poor visibility.
1) _____ ?
2) _____ ?

 Magnetic compass. The compass shows the aircraft's heading relative to Magnetic North. While reliable in steady level flight it can give confusing indications when turning, climbing, descending or accelerating due to the inclination of the Earth's magnetic field. For this reason, the heading indicator is also used for aircraft operation.
1) _____ ?
2) _____ ?

 Turn indicator. The turn indicator displays the direction of turn and rate of turn. An internally mounted inclinometer displays the "quality" of turn, i.e. whether the turn is correctly coordinated.
1) _____ ?
2) _____ ?

Heading indicator. The heading indicator (also known as the directional gyro, or DG; sometimes also called the gyrocompass, though usually not in aviation applications) displays the aircraft's heading with respect to Geographical North.
1) _____ ?
2) _____ ?

6 **Read the text and label the picture, writing the numbers in the right circles, according to the description.**

Most aircraft are equipped with a standard set of flight instruments which give the pilot information about the aircraft's attitude, airspeed and altitude. They have at least four of the flight instruments located in a standardised pattern called the T arrangement.

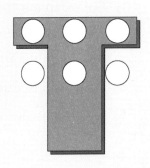

The attitude indicator (1) is in the top center, airspeed (2) to the left, altimeter (3) to the right and heading indicator (4) under the attitude indicator. The other two, turn-coordinator (5) and vertical-speed (6), are usually found under the airspeed and altimeter.

Reading 2

The bridge

The room from which a ship is commanded is known as the **bridge**. In this room there are usually three or more men working to control the ship's movements: the captain, an OOW — officer of the watch, an AB — able seaman, and a pilot. Like many other forms of transport, the direction of the ship is controlled by a **steering** wheel located on the bridge. The **throttle** — which provides the forward and backward movement of the **vessel**, is also controlled from this area. On all ships **visibility** is **obviously** very important, both for safe **navigation** and, in the case of **warships**, to be able to see the enemy. On most modern ships the bridge is in a high position and provides a near 360° **view**.

MY GLOSSARY

bridge	n.	（舰船的）驾驶台，船桥，舰桥
steer	v.	掌舵；驾驶
throttle	n.	节流阀
vessel	n.	船，舰
visibility	n.	能见度，可见性

obviously	adv.	明显地，显然地
navigation	n.	航行，航海
warship	n.	战舰，军舰
view	n.	视野；风景

7 Read the text and decide if these statements are true (*T*) or false (*F*).

	T	F
1) On a ship the "bridge" is a type of room.	☐	☐
2) The direction of a ship is not controlled by a wheel.	☐	☐
3) The ship's throttle is controlled from a different area.	☐	☐
4) On warships visibility is important for two reasons.	☐	☐
5) From the bridge it is possible to see all around.	☐	☐

8 Find the synonyms of these words from the text.

1) controlled   _____

2) positioned   _____

3) vehicle   _____

4) panorama   _____

5) cruising   _____

Reading 3

The signal box

You are probably familiar with the small buildings standing next to railway lines, but possibly do not know what they are used for. These constructions are known as **signal boxes** or **switch towers**, and were **fundamental** for the development of the railway system. The signal box was first used in the mid-19th century, and was a space for **signalmen** to control the direction of trains and ensure the safety of passengers and vehicles. At first, this job was carried out manually by moving **levers** to move the **track**, but with the invention of electrical and electronic technology, the signalman's job changed **radically**. First, he was able to control much larger areas of track from a **control panel**, and could communicate directly with trains by radio or telephone, and later he was able to **perform** all of these tasks by computer. **Eventually**, the signal box fell into **disuse**. Today most signaling is controlled centrally by very **sophisticated** computers, but for many years the simple signal box guaranteed safe rail travel all over the world; and perhaps many of these little buildings still exist to remind us of their important role in the development of the railway system.

The signal box inn

In the Cleethorpes region of Great Britain, there is a very unusual signal box that is now used for something completely different. The Signal Box Inn is a pub; in fact, at only 6 m², it is in the Guinness Book of Records as the smallest pub in the world, with room inside for only 6 people! Although it is very small, it serves 5 types of beer and cider and some food. The best place to enjoy your drink while you watch steam trains go by is in the pub's beer garden.

MY GLOSSARY

signal	*n.*	信号
	v.	用信号通知; 表示
signal box		信号房, 信号箱
switch tower		信号塔
fundamental	*adj.*	基本的, 根本的
signalman	*n.*	信号员, 通信兵
lever	*n.*	控制杆, 杠杆
track	*n.*	轨道; 小道

radically	*adv.*	根本地, 彻底地
control panel		控制面板
perform	*v.*	执行, 完成
eventually	*adv.*	最后, 终于
disuse	*n.*	停止使用, 不被使用
sophisticated	*adj.*	复杂的, 精密的; 世故的; 高级的

9 Read the text and answer the questions.

1) What was the function of the signal box?

2) What innovations changed the job of the signalman?

3) How did the signalman communicate with trains?

4) Why are signal boxes no longer in use?

5) Why do signal boxes still exist?

10 Match these words or phrases with their definitions.

1) switch points   a ☐ protection from danger

2) heritage   b ☐ long handles used to operate machinery

3) safety   c ☐ pieces of railway line that can be moved to change the direction of a train

4) control panel   d ☐ the history and traditions of a country

5) levers   e ☐ a flat board on machinery containing instruments

Listening

11 **Listen to the description of a cab and complete the text.**

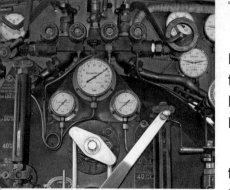

The cab

    Propulsion for the train is provided by a (1) _____ **locomotive**, or by individual (2) _____ in **self-propelled** multiple units. Most modern trains are powered by (3) _____ locomotives or by **electricity supplied** by **overhead** wires or (4) _____ rails, although historically the steam locomotive was the **dominant** form of locomotive (5) _____ .

    The cab, **crew** compartment or driver's compartment, is the part of the locomotive housing the (6) _____ and the controls necessary for the locomotive's operation. On steam locomotives, the cab is normally (7) _____ to the **rear** of the **firebox**. The cab of a **diesel** or electric locomotive is either (8) _____ a cabin or forming one of the **structural** elements of a cab unit locomotive.

MY GLOSSARY

propulsion	*n.*	驱动力, 推进力	crew	*n.*	全体人员; 队, 组
locomotive	*n.*	机车, 火车头			
self-propelled	*adj.*	自行驱动的, 自推进的	rear	*n.*	后面
electricity	*n.*	电力, 电流	firebox	*n.*	防火箱
supply	*v.*	供给, 提供	diesel	*n.*	柴油机
overhead	*adj.*	在空中, 在头顶上	structural	*adj.*	结构的; 建筑的
dominant	*adj.*	主要的; 占优势的, 支配的			

Speaking

12 **Ask and answer the questions in pairs.**

1) Would you like to become a driver?

2) Would you prefer to drive a lorry or a train? Why?

3) Which one of these two means of transport do you think is more difficult to drive? Why?

Technical Terms

Formula One	一级方程式赛车
OOW (officer of the watch)	值班驾驶员
AB (able seaman)	一等水手，熟练水手

UNIT 3 Positioning Tools

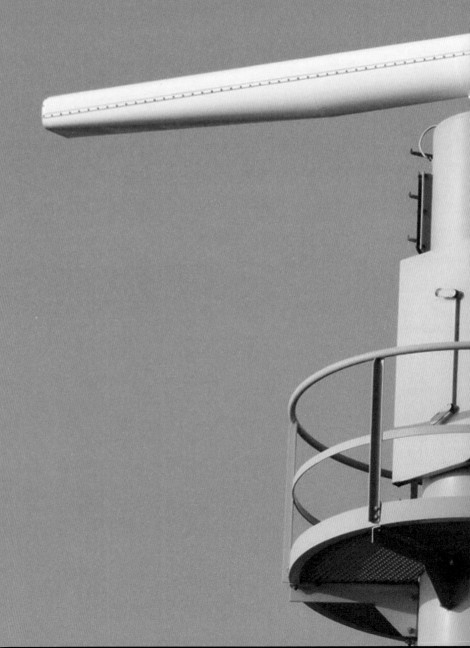

Learning Objectives

Upon completion of the unit, students will be able to:

• identify different technologies in positioning and how they work;

• master the words and expressions related to positioning;

• compare the advantages and disadvantages of different positioning tools.

Starting Off

1 **Write each means of positioning under the picture.**

GPS System　　radar　　compass　　China's BeiDou Navigation Satellite System (BDS)

1) _____

2) _____

3) _____

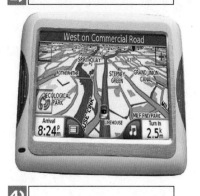

4) _____

Reading 1

From using the sun, the moon and the stars to the development of compasses and maps and in very recent times the technology of satellite GPS Systems and **radar**, man has always needed a way to find his **bearings**, whether travelling on foot, at sea or in the air. **Navigation** is as fundamental for humans today as it was in the past, and with all the sophisticated technology now available navigation tools are not just used to stop people getting lost.

Consider the transport industry for example. A GPS **tracking system** on a truck can ensure that a driver takes the best route—avoiding traffic, saving time and **petrol** costs—but it also helps the transport company to **monitor** the driver and ensure that he respects the **speed limits**, only travels at the permitted times and rests at regular **intervals** for the required amount of time, respecting the law and increasing safety. It can even allow the company to find the vehicle **in case of** theft!

You have probably used maps on the Internet or your mobile phone, and have seen how satellite **images** can now **identify** places with **incredible** detail, even looking into your living room from the sky above! This can be useful for planning a trip before you leave or finding a friend's house; but the technology is also used for **a** whole **series of professional** purposes: from **calculating** weather to **urban planning** and even security and **warfare**.

Like all forms of technology the GPS has a few disadvantages of course—it is not always 100% **reliable**—the suggested route may not always be the best, because some problems are not signaled or the information **transmitted** to the map is not completely accurate; and some people consider that GPS is an **invasion** of their **privacy**. However, this technology is obviously here to stay, and **destined** to improve; and, if used properly, its advantages are clearly greater than its drawbacks.

MY GLOSSARY

radar	n.	雷达	incredible	adj.	难以置信的
bearing	n.	方位，方位角	a series of		一系列的，一连串的
navigation	n.	导航，领航	professional	adj.	专业的，职业的
tracking system		跟踪系统，追踪系统	calculate	v.	计算；预测
petrol	n.	汽油	urban planning		城市规划
monitor	v.	监控，监测	warfare	n.	战争，冲突
speed limit		（道路的）最高时速限制，限速	reliable	adj.	可靠的，可信赖的
			transmit	v.	传输，传送
interval	n.	间隔，间距	invasion	n.	侵犯，侵扰，入侵
in case of		万一，如果	privacy	n.	隐私，秘密
image	n.	影像，图像	destined	adj.	注定的；有特定目的地的
identify	v.	确定，识别			

2 Read the text and answer the questions.

1) What tools did man use for navigating before the invention of satellite technology?

2) How can GPS Systems help truck drivers?

3) Can you name some of the legal advantages of GPS for the transport industry?

4) What example is given of the accuracy of satellite images?

5) Why do some people not like this technology?

3 Match these words with their definitions.

1) bearing   **a** ☐ disadvantage

2) tracking   **b** ☐ activity of fighting war

3) safety   **c** ☐ direction from a fixed point, e.g. by using a compass

4) theft   **d** ☐ protecting things and people from danger

5) security   **e** ☐ the crime of stealing things

6) warfare   **f** ☐ following the movements of something

7) drawback   **g** ☐ not being in danger

Reading 2

The radar

The word RADAR stands for Radio **Detection** and **Ranging**. It is a technology which was properly used for the first time during the Second World War by **the allied troops** against the Germans.

Basically, a radar is an **anti-collision** tool and can measure the bearing and the distance of a selected target. It is therefore a vital aid on ships and airplanes, especially in case of low or blind-visibility navigation.

To detect a target's position the radar dish or **antenna** sends out **pulses** of **electromagnetic waves**. When these waves hit the target, their **echo** is returned to the **aerial** and **transformed** into **visual** signals shown on a screen called PPI (Plan Position Indicator) or display. The capacity of the antenna to concentrate the **irradiation** energy in the dish is called **gain**. The whole process is based on the principle that radio waves **bounce off** solid surfaces. It is therefore possible to determine the bearings and distances of faraway targets and **deduce** information about potential **hazards**. The radar can also be used to find out the position of a ship at sea, but only in the case in which a **fix** (a fixed point of reference on the land) is available. For this, other more **precise**, handy and faster tools, like the GPS, are used.

detection	n.	探测, 侦查		transform	v.	转化, 改变
ranging	n.	测距		visual	adj.	视觉的, 视力的
the allied troop		盟军		irradiation	n.	照射, 发光
anti-collision	adj.	防冲撞的, 防冲突的		gain	n.	输入信号增益控制; 获得
antenna	n.	天线; 触角		bounce off		反射, 弹开
pulse	n.	脉冲; 脉搏		deduce	v.	推论, 推断
electromagnetic wave		电磁波		hazard	n.	危险, 危害
echo	n.	反射; 回声		fix	n.	固定方位, 定位
aerial	n.	天线		precise	adj.	准确的, 确切的
	adj.	空中的, 空气的				

4 Read the text and answer the questions.

1) What does the word RADAR mean?

2) When was it properly used for the first time?

3) What type of wave does it make use of?

4) What is the working principle of the radar?

5) Can you define the term "gain"?

6) What is a fix?

5 Look at the chart and match the following acronyms with their definitions.

Radar plotting is the set of calculations and graphics of naval kinematics.
They are used to trace the positions of moving targets detected by the radar.
This is a plotting chart paper filled in with data by a student.

Acronym		Definitions
1) RMIL	a ☐	Own Ship
2) RMIPL	b ☐	Close Point of Approach (the point in which the two ships will be nearest)
3) OS	c ☐	Another Ship
4) AS	d ☐	Relative Motion Indicator Parallel Line
5) CPA	e ☐	Point in which AS passes in front of OS's bow
6) BP (Bow Passage)	f ☐	Relative Motion Indicator Line

The GPS System

A ☐ GPS, which stands for Global Positioning System, is a radio navigation system belonging to the **American Ministry of Defense**, that allows land, sea, and **airborne** users to determine their exact location, **velocity**, and time 24 hours a day, in all weather conditions, anywhere in the world.

B ☐ The complete name of the system is NAVSTAR GPS, which means "Navigation Satellite Timing and Ranging Global Positioning System". It was born as a top secret project of the American Department of Defense during the final years of **the Cold War** so **initially** it was intended just for military purposes.

C ☐ Today the GPS service is provided free of charge by the United States Air Force to the entire world. It is a **constellation** of satellites (21 active and 3 spare ones) **orbiting** at 11,000 **nautical miles** above the Earth and a series of ground stations that control and monitor those satellites. The satellites are **spaced** so that from any point on Earth, four satellites will be above the **horizon**.

D ☐ On the ground, any GPS receiver contains a computer that "**triangulates**" its own position by getting bearings from three of the four satellites. The result is provided in the form of a **geographic** position — **longitude** and **latitude** — for most receivers, within a few metres. If the receiver is also equipped with a display screen that shows a map, the position can be shown on the map. When a fourth satellite can be received, the receiver/computer can calculate the altitude as well as the geographic position. If you are moving, your receiver may also be able to calculate your speed and direction of travel and give you estimated times of arrival to **specified destinations**.

MY GLOSSARY

American Ministry of Defense		美国国防部
airborne	*adj.*	在空中飞的; 空运的; 空气传播的
velocity	*n.*	速度; 高速
the Cold War		冷战
initially	*adv.*	最初, 首先
constellation	*n.*	星座
orbit	*v.*	沿轨道运行; 围绕……运动
	n.	轨道
nautical mile		海里

space	*v.*	以一定间隔排列
horizon	*n.*	地平线; 视野
triangulate	*v.*	用三角测量法测定（高度、距离、方位）
geographic	*adj.*	地理的; 地理学的
longitude	*n.*	经度, 经线
latitude	*n.*	纬度, 纬线
specified	*adj.*	规定的; 特定的
destination	*n.*	目的地, 终点

6 Read the text and choose the best title for each paragraph (A–D).

1) History of the GPS

2) Function of the ground stations

3) The meaning and functioning of the GPS

4) GPS satellites

7 Decide if these statements are true (*T*) or false (*F*). Correct the false ones.

	T	F
1) The GPS System is the property of each country in which it is used.	☐	☐
2) The GPS System cannot be used in the air.	☐	☐
3) At the beginning it was used as a military tool.	☐	☐
4) The use of the GPS System is free.	☐	☐
5) The GPS System is made up of more than 20 satellites.	☐	☐

8 Paraphrase the following words and expressions.

1) radio navigation system _____

2) location _____

3) provide _____

4) ground station _____

5) equip _____

9 Look at the picture and then answer the questions.

1) How many satellites is the GPS appliance currently receiving?

2) What is the speed of the vehicle?

3) What is its final destination?

4) What is its next foreseen change of direction?

5) How long will it take?

Listening

10 Listen to this extract about the radar history and complete the text.

We see everything because of reflected (1) _____. Radar is a **beam**, not of visible light, but of a related form of (2) _____: **microwave radiation**. When an invisible beam of microwaves is directed outwards and something crosses its path, a little of the microwave energy is bounced back to its (3) _____. The time it takes a pulse of microwave energy to travel out and be (4) _____ back, allows us to understand the distance from the object being tracked. The (5) _____ of the returning energy, coming back to the radar, gives the (6) _____ of the object. In 1935 **Nazi dictator** Adolf Hitler **announced** the rebirth of the German Air Force, the Luftwaffe. Anxious to protect their cities from the threat of German bombing, the British Government **commissioned** the Scottish radio (7) _____ Robert Watson Watt to **investigate** the possibility of creating a death ray to shoot down Nazi aircraft. Watson Watt took the ideas for a death (8) _____ and turned them into the world's first practical radar system. RADAR stands for Radio Detection and Ranging. Before 1935 radars were (9) _____ and could only detect very large objects like a ship. In that year, Robert Watson Watt made a **crucial breakthrough**. He devised a radar that could **spot** something as small as an (10) _____, applying scientific principles already well understood at the time.

MY GLOSSARY

beam	*n.*	（电波的）波束; 光线	commission	*v.*	委托, 委任
microwave	*n.*	微波; 微波炉	investigate	*v.*	研究, 调查
radiation	*n.*	辐射; 放射线	crucial	*adj.*	至关重要的, 关键性的
Nazi	*n.*	纳粹党人, 纳粹分子	breakthrough	*n.*	重大进展, 突破
dictator	*n.*	独裁者	spot	*v.*	发现, 注意到
announce	*v.*	宣布, 宣告			

11 Listen and complete the text with the missing numbers.

You know that **incredibly uncomfortable** feeling you get when you realise you are totally lost, for example in the woods or on the open ocean or in an unfamiliar city. With the Global Positioning System you can know exactly where you are, anywhere on the planet. All you need is a small **hand-held** receiver.

The system that makes it work is **absolutely** amazing. There are (1) _____ GPS satellites in orbit. They fly at an altitude of (2) _____ miles and there are always (3) _____ or (4) _____ of them overhead at any time. To find your location your receiver calculates exactly how far away it is from at least (5) _____ overhead satellites.

Then it uses a little **trigonometry**. If you **intersect** (6) _____ **spheres** you get a circle. If you intersect (7) _____ spheres you get (8) _____ points. The Earth is a sphere. So if you have only (9) _____ satellites you can use the Earth as (10) _____ of the spheres.

Since most GPS receivers have maps built in, you can use your longitude and latitude to find your way out of the woods, to the shore or to your favourite restaurant.

MY GLOSSARY

incredibly	*adv.*	非常, 极其, 难以置信地
uncomfortable	*adj.*	不舒服的, 不安的
hand-held	*adj.*	便携式的, 手提式的
absolutely	*adv.*	绝对地, 完全地

trigonometry	*n.*	三角学
intersect	*v.*	横切; 贯穿; 相交, 交叉
sphere	*n.*	球体, 球, 球形

Writing

12 **Provide a short and simple explanation for each of the following proverbs. The first one is done for you.**

1) Check the course first and then loosen the sails.
This proverb means that before sailing you must check your direction and destination carefully.

2) If there is snow, mist or thick fog, be careful and slow and listen to signals.

_____

_____

3) We've been beneath the radar all year.

_____

_____

4) It is certainly on our radar for priority.

_____

_____

Technical Terms

China's BeiDou Navigation Satellite System (BDS)　　中国北斗导航系统

Radio Detection and Ranging (RADAR)　　雷达，无线电探测和测距

PPI (Plan Position Indicator)　　平面位置显示器

NAVSTAR GPS (Navigation Satellite Timing
and Ranging Global Positioning System)　　导航星，全球定位系统（GPS的全称）

UNIT 4 What's the Weather Like?

Learning Objectives

Upon completion of the unit, students will be able to:

• identify different weather prediction tools;

• master the words and expressions related to weather prediction;

• understand the importance of weather forecast to transport.

Unit 4   What's the Weather Like?   39

Starting Off

Of all human activities, transport is probably one of the most **influenced** by the weather. From deciding whether or not to go for a walk in the park to **cancelling** or **delaying intercontinental passenger flights**, the weather influences our movements all the time. Extreme weather conditions can cause accidents, death and **destruction** so **predicting** the weather is a **priority** when people and goods are moved from one place to another. Today man has developed some very sophisticated means for predicting the weather, but despite this, our **predictions** are not always accurate because weather conditions can change very suddenly.

MY GLOSSARY

influence	v.	影响; 对……起作用	destruction	n.	破坏, 毁灭
cancel	v.	取消, 撤销	predict	v.	预测, 预报
delay	v.	延期; 耽搁	priority	n.	优先事项, 最重要的事
intercontinental	adj.	洲际的, 洲与洲之间的	prediction	n.	预测, 预报
passenger flight		客机			

1 **Match the icons with the weather conditions.**

1)   a ☐ partially cloudy

2)   b ☐ snowy

3)   c ☐ rainy

4)   d ☐ cloudy

5)   e ☐ sunny

6)   f ☐ frosty

7)   g ☐ stormy

2 **Label these weather forecast symbols with the expressions from the box.**

> wind direction   wind force   marine forecast   maximum temperature   minimum temperature

1) _____

2) _____

3) _____

4) _____

5) _____

Listening

3 Listen and complete the table with the correct information.

	Weather	Pressure	Wind direction	Wind force
Tonight		Low 59		10 to 20 mph
Saturday morning				15 to 25 mph
Saturday night		Low 44	/	/

4 Listen to the question "What's the weather like today?" and fill in the table with as many adjectives as you can.

Sight	Touch/Feeling	Temperature	Opinion
cloudy	windy	cool	wonderful

Speaking

5 Work in pairs. Find a weather forecast map from the Internet and talk about it. You can refer to the following questions for help.

1) What is the weather going to be like in your city?

2) Which is the hottest part of the area?

3) Which is the coldest part of the area?

4) Is there an area of high pressure?

5) Are there going to be thunderstorms/snow/rain/frost?

6) Can you describe the temperature and general conditions of a certain place in the map?

Reading 1

6 Read the text and match the paragraphs with the pictures.

1) ☐ Have you ever been in a situation when the **weather forecast** predicted sunny skies, but then it rained all day? You think, "Oh no, I wish I had my umbrella!"

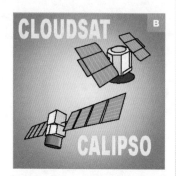

2) ☐ The job of predicting weather accurately is a difficult one, because our atmosphere is **constantly** changing. Weather **forecasters** must **analyse** information they receive from a number of **sources**, including mobile weather **observers**, **weather balloons**, **weather stations** and satellites.

3) ☐ NASA uses a series of satellites called the Afternoon Constellation, **nicknamed** the "A-Train", which are orbiting in air and are collecting all sorts of data, including those that will help predict weather and climate changes.

the "A-Train"

4) ☐ Two additional satellites, **Cloudsat** and **Calipso**, will soon be **launched** to **extend** the series. Cloudsat will help improve weather forecasting, by studying the different aspects of clouds, as it name **implies**. Calipso will help predict climate change and how **aerosols** or **particles** affect the Earth's atmosphere.

5) ☐ We **rely on** weather predictions for many activities:
■ farmers need to know the best time to plant and **harvest** their crops;
■ airplanes' take-offs, landings and flight plans are **scheduled** according to local weather conditions;
■ weather forecasters warn newspapers about severe storms that could **endanger** life or **property**.

Most people want to know what the weather will be like as they go to and from work or school, or plan outdoor activities; but although we receive weather data from such **a** great **variety of** sources, we know that it is still impossible to predict the weather accurately 100% of the time.

weather forecast		天气预报
constantly	adv.	不断地, 时常地
forecaster	n.	预报员
analyse	v.	分析
source	n.	来源; 起源, 根源
observer	n.	观测者; 目击者
weather balloon		气象探测气球
weather station		气象站
nickname	v.	给……起绰号
	n.	绰号
Cloudsat	n.	云探测卫星
Calipso	n.	卡利普索激光雷达卫星

launch	v.	发射; 发起
extend	v.	扩大; 延伸
imply	v.	暗示, 暗指
aerosol	n.	气溶胶
particle	n.	微粒, 颗粒
rely on		依靠, 依赖
harvest	v.	收割, 收获
schedule	v.	安排; 预定
	n.	计划表, 时间表
endanger	v.	危及, 危害
property	n.	财产; 性能
a variety of		各种各样的

7 Read the text again and answer the questions.

1) Why is it so difficult to predict the weather?

2) Where do weather forecasters get their information?

3) Where is the "A-train" and what does it do?

4) Why are two new satellites being launched?

5) What do farmers need the weather forecast for?

8 Find the synonyms of these words or phrases from the text.

1) precisely _____

2) interpret _____

3) group _____

4) predicting _____

5) depend on _____

6) serious _____

7) planned _____

Reading 2

Severe weather conditions can be dangerous for aircraft

Ice **buildup** on the wings, tail and **stabilisers** of an aircraft may be very dangerous, because it can change the way air flows around them, slowing the plane and **compromising** the wings' ability to lift the plane as it moves forward.

Two different processes are used to try and solve this problem: **de-icing** and **anti-icing**.

De-icing is the removal of existing snow, ice, frost, etc., from a surface.

Anti-icing is the **application** of **chemicals** that not only de-ice, but remain on a surface and continue to delay the **reformation** of ice up to a certain period of time, or prevent **adhesion** of ice to make **mechanical** removal easier.

Frost, ice or snow on **critical** surfaces of an aircraft such as wings, **propellers** and stabilisers can have a significant **impact** on the operation of an aircraft. The aircraft can be affected in two ways:

- the formation of frost, ice or snow changes the **airflow** over the wing, reducing lift and increasing drag;
- the **additional** weight of the ice or snow adds to the total weight of the aircraft, increasing the lift required for the aircraft to take off. The **combination** of reduced lift, increased drag and increased weight from even small quantities of ice, snow or frost, can **affect performance** and **handling**, which can have **dramatic consequences**.

De-icing is **performed** by **spraying** heated Type 1 **glycol** aircraft de-icing fluid (ADF) on frost, snow and ice to **melt** and remove them from the critical surfaces. If **precipitation** continues after the Type 1 application, then a non-heated Type 4 glycol aircraft anti-icing fluid (AAF) application is necessary to prevent further buildup before take-off.

MY GLOSSARY

buildup	*n.*	集结, 增长	adhesion	*n.*	粘附(力), 粘着
stabiliser	*n.*	稳定器, 平衡器	mechanical	*adj.*	机械的; 力学的
compromise	*v.*	损害	critical	*adj.*	极重要的, 关键的
de-icing	*n.*	除冰	propeller	*n.*	螺旋桨; 推进器
anti-icing	*n.*	防冰	impact	*n.*	影响, 作用
application	*n.*	应用, 运用	airflow	*n.*	气流
chemical	*n.*	化学制品, 化学品	additional	*adj.*	附加的, 额外的
reformation	*n.*	再次形成; 改革, 革新	combination	*n.*	组合, 结合, 联合

affect	v.	影响	spray	v.	喷, 喷洒
performance	n.	性能; 表现; 表演	glycol	n.	乙二醇, 甘醇
handling	n.	操作; 处理	melt	v.	融化; 熔化; 溶解
dramatic	adj.	巨大的; 剧烈的	precipitation	n.	（尤指雨或雪的）降落, 降水; 沉淀
consequence	n.	后果; 结果			
perform	v.	完成; 执行			

9 Read the text and answer the questions.

1) Why can ice building up on aircraft parts be dangerous?

2) What actions can be taken against ice buildup on aircraft?

3) In what ways can ice buildup affect the aircraft?

4) How is de-icing carried out?

5) When is AAF used?

10 Complete these sentences with information from the text.

1) When ice forms on an aircraft, it can change the way the air flows around the _____, _____ and _____.

2) When the airflow over the plane's wing is changed by ice, it _____ drag and _____ lift.

3) When the total weight of an aircraft is increased by the presence of ice, it means that _____.

4) The difference between the two safety procedures applied in these conditions is that _____.

11 Match these words with their definitions.

1) ice   a ☐ a powered, fixed-wing aircraft

2) plane   b ☐ a solid deposit of water vapour

3) snow   c ☐ liquid that continually flows

4) frost   d ☐ frozen water

5) fluid   e ☐ small, soft, frozen water that falls from the sky

12 **Match these English weather proverbs with their explanations.**

1) Red sky at night, sailor's delight.

2) Clear moon, frost soon.

3) Rainbow in the morning gives you fair warning.

4) Lightning never strikes the same place twice.

5) Halo around the sun or moon, rain or snow soon.

6) Red sky in the morning, sailors take warning.

a ☐ A red sky during sunrise indicates that a storm is possible.

b ☐ There is a shower to the West on its way.

c ☐ When the sky is red at sunset, good weather is predicted for the following day.

d ☐ Halo or ring indicates moisture in the upper atmosphere, so it is thought that moisture is on its way down in the form of precipitation.

e ☐ A false myth which states that lightning never falls a second time in the same place.

f ☐ When there is no cloud cover at night, the air temperature will cool more quickly, hence greater chance of frost in the morning.

Writing

13 **Do you know any other proverbs related to weather? Try to translate them into English, maintaining rhymes when possible. Use a dictionary and ask your teacher for help. Then explain them in plain English.**

Technical Terms

NASA (National Aeronautics and Space Administration)	（美国）国家航空和航天局
aircraft de-icing fluid (ADF)	飞机除冻液
aircraft anti-icing fluid (AAF)	飞机防冻液

UNIT 5 Intermodal Freight Transport

Learning Objectives

Upon completion of the unit, students will be able to:

• identify the functions of intermodal freight transport;

• master the words and expressions related to intermodal freight transport;

• understand the advantages of intermodal freight transport.

Starting Off

1 **Match the following transport modal shifts with the right pictures.**

1) Ship to lorry

2) Lorry to warehouse

3) Train to lorry

4) Airplane to lorry

 A □

 B □

 C □

 D □

Reading 1

Transport is everywhere! In the air, by rail or road, on the water, by **cable** or **pipeline** and even in space—people, animals and goods are constantly **on the move**. Transport is fundamental both for trade between people and for **establishing cultural exchanges** and increasing understanding between different cultures. As a field of study transport can be divided into three **categories**: **infrastructure**, vehicles and **operations**. Infrastructure for transport is all around us—from airports, railway and bus stations to **warehouses**, **trucking terminals**, **refueling depots** and **seaports**. Vehicles include **automobiles**, bicycles, buses, trains, trucks, people, ships, **helicopters** and airplanes. Operations deal with the way the vehicles are operated, and the **procedures** set for this purpose, including **financing**, **legalities** and **policies**. Passenger transport may be public or private. Freight transport is today focused on **containerisation**. Transport plays an important part in economic growth and **globalisation**, but can also cause air pollution and use large amounts of land. It is **commonly** heavily influenced by governments, both in terms of **subsidies** and planning, which is **essential** to make traffic flow and control urban **sprawl**.

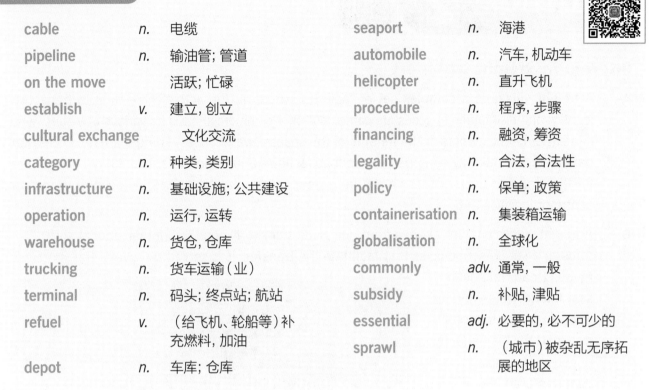

cable	n.	电缆
pipeline	n.	输油管; 管道
on the move		活跃; 忙碌
establish	v.	建立, 创立
cultural exchange		文化交流
category	n.	种类, 类别
infrastructure	n.	基础设施; 公共建设
operation	n.	运行, 运转
warehouse	n.	货仓, 仓库
trucking	n.	货车运输（业）
terminal	n.	码头; 终点站; 航站
refuel	v.	（给飞机、轮船等）补充燃料, 加油
depot	n.	车库; 仓库
seaport	n.	海港
automobile	n.	汽车, 机动车
helicopter	n.	直升飞机
procedure	n.	程序, 步骤
financing	n.	融资, 筹资
legality	n.	合法, 合法性
policy	n.	保单; 政策
containerisation	n.	集装箱运输
globalisation	n.	全球化
commonly	adv.	通常, 一般
subsidy	n.	补贴, 津贴
essential	adj.	必要的, 必不可少的
sprawl	n.	（城市）被杂乱无序拓展的地区

2 Read the text and answer the questions.

1) What are the most common forms of transport?

2) Why is transport so important?

3) What are the most common forms of infrastructure for land-based transport?

4) Can you name two problems that can result from the transport industry?

5) What areas do governments need to influence in the transport industry?

3 Match these words with their definitions.

1) cable   a ☐ the systems and services necessary for a country to function well

2) goods   b ☐ a place where goods are stored

3) infrastructure   c ☐ the fact of being allowed by law

4) depot   d ☐ thick, strong metal rope or wire

5) legality   e ☐ the process of transporting goods in enormous boxes

6) containerisation   f ☐ to move smoothly and constantly

7) subsidy   g ☐ products destined for sale, carried by truck, plane or ship

8) flow   h ☐ money that governments give to help organisations

Reading 2

Intermodal freight transport

A ☐ A **freight village** is **a complex set of facilities** where all the activities relating to transport, logistics and **distribution** of goods are carried out on a **commercial** basis by **various operators**, who can either be the owners or the **tenants** of the spaces (warehouses, **storage areas**, offices, car parks, etc.). It must be equipped with public facilities and, if possible, include public services for the staff and users. Other names for a freight village are: logistics park/centre, transport centre or logistics **hub**.

B ☐ A freight village enables change from one given transport mode to another (**modal shift**) through a set of technologies that **facilitate** the **transfer**. It is served by several transport modes (road, rail, deep sea, **inland waterway**, air) to encourage intermodal transport for the handling of goods.The most common examples of modal shifts are: train (rail) to lorry (road); **barge** (inland waterway) to train or lorry; airplane (air) to lorry.

C ☐ A freight village requires different activities such as warehousing, economic activities, support activities and **unified** management. The warehouse is the infrastructure where the transport operator mostly performs his business. This activity may include the **division** of the goods into smaller quantities for a more **functional** distribution. Logistics hubs need active distribution centres and several industrial activities in the **neighbourhood** that can **exploit** the modal shift facilities within the village. Support activities include support services like lorry rest areas, office space, restaurants, banking, shops and hotels. Unified management requires that the village is often under the management of a single **entity**.

D ☐ A freight village is the right **solution** to satisfy the increasing requirements of a complex business based on transport. In order to work well it is **imperative** that the village is run by a single body, either public or private.

freight village		货运村	facilitate	v.	促进, 帮助
a set of		一套, 一组	transfer	n. / v.	转移; 转让
complex	adj.	复杂的; 让人费解的	inland waterway		内陆水道, 内陆航道
facility	n.	设施, 设备	barge	n.	驳船, 平底载货船
distribution	n.	配送, 发送	unified	adj.	统一的, 一致的
commercial	adj.	商业的, 商务的	division	n.	分配; 分配方法
various	adj.	各种各样的	functional	adj.	功能性的; 实用的
operator	n.	经营者; 专业公司	neighbourhood	n.	邻近地区; 街区
tenant	n.	承租人, 租户	exploit	v.	利用; 开发
storage area		储物区, 货仓	entity	n.	实体, 独立存在体
hub	n.	中心, 枢纽	solution	n.	解决办法, 解决方案
modal shift		运输方式转换	imperative	adj.	极重要的, 必要的

4 **Read the text and choose the best title for each paragraph (A–D).**

1) Description of the main activities of a freight village

2) Introduction to the concept of freight village

3) Final statement on a freight village

4) Extra information on freight villages

5 **Read the text and write _T_ (True), _F_ (False) or _DS_ (Doesn't say).**

1) A freight village is also called a logistics hub. _____

2) A modal shift train to airplane is not possible. _____

3) In the warehouse goods are usually assembled in bigger quantities. _____

4) In a freight village there are never banks or restaurants. _____

5) A freight village is usually run by a single person. _____

Oil tankers

The **oil tanker** was developed in the late 19th century as a solution for transporting large quantities of "**black gold**" across the globe. Today, oil tankers fall into two basic categories, **crude tankers** and product tankers. Crude tankers are the larger of the two. They move **raw**, **unrefined** oil from the places where it's **pumped** out of the earth, to the **refineries** where it is **processed** into **fuel** and other products. Product tankers, on the other hand, are smaller than crude tankers and move already-processed **petroleum** products to markets where they can be sold and used. **Corporations** are always seeking the most efficient way to **accomplish** a task in order to **maximise** profits. Due to their immense size, oil tankers provide an easy and inexpensive way to transport oil over long distances. In fact, it only costs around two to four cents per **gallon** to transport oil using a **typical** tanker. Like many other **influential** technologies, oil tankers have helped us progress as a **civilisation**, but they have also presented us with **considerable** problems. Without oil tankers, it would be impossible to travel as easily and often as we do. However, some of the worst man-made environmental disasters in history have resulted from oil tanker accidents. When oil **spills** into the sea, it creates enormous damage to nature, which takes many years to recover. In order to prevent these accidents occurring again in the future, new **regulations** have been introduced. For example, new oil tankers must be **double-hulled**, which means that there are two **layers** separating the oil they carry from the sea. This reduces the risk of oil spills in case the tanker has an accident, but of course it does not **eliminate** risk completely. Sea transportation of oil also carries other risks, including **pirates**, who take control of the tanker and demand money in return. The future of oil tankers is also uncertain, just as the future of the oil industry itself is. Man is looking for new ways of producing energy as oil **reserves** are finishing and **ecological issues** are becoming more important.

oil tanker		油轮
black gold		黑金（特指石油）
crude tanker		原油油轮
raw	*adj.*	未经加工的; 生的
unrefined	*adj.*	未提炼的, 未精制的
pump	*v.*	用泵（或泵样器官或设备等）输送
refinery	*n.*	炼油厂
process	*v.*	加工, 处理
fuel	*n.*	燃油, 燃料
petroleum	*n.*	石油
corporation	*n.*	公司, 企业
accomplish	*v.*	完成, 实现
maximise	*v.*	使最大化; 使最重要
gallon	*n.*	加仑（液体计量单位）

typical	*adj.*	典型的; 特有的
influential	*adj.*	有影响力的
civilisation	*n.*	文明, 文化
considerable	*adj.*	相当多（大、重要）的
spill	*v.*	（使）洒出; （使）溢出
	n.	洒出（量）; 溢出（量）
regulation	*n.*	规则, 法规
double-hulled	*adj.*	双重机壳的, 双壳体的
layer	*n.*	层; 层次
eliminate	*v.*	消除, 排除
pirate	*n.*	海盗
reserve	*n.*	储备（物）, 备用（物）
ecological	*adj.*	生态的; 生态学的
issue	*n.*	问题; 议题

6 Read the text and answer the questions.

1) Why were oil tankers developed?

2) What is the main difference between the two types of oil tanker?

3) What are the main advantages of oil tankers as a form of transportation?

4) What are the main disadvantages?

5) Why is the future of oil tankers uncertain?

Listening

Air freight

Today an increasing number of goods are transported by air. Planes can transport letters, cars and even horses as well as other planes! Virtually every passenger flight also transports cargo, and of course many flights are for the transportation of goods only. The planes used may be similar to passenger planes or are sometimes old passenger planes which have been converted for goods transportation, or they may be cargo aircraft, some of which are enormous. The Boeing 747-400, for example, can transport the same quantity of goods as 5 articulated lorries! But there is yet another category of plane which was developed exclusively for cargo: the super transporter. The largest of these, the Antonov AN-225, can carry over 250 tons of cargo!

7 **Complete the table referring to the text above with the words or terms from the box. Then listen and check.**

| Russia | Europe | two | Super Guppy | four | USA | four | Antonov |
| four | Airbus | six | 747 Dreamlifter | USA | 124) | Antonov | |

		Aircraft and company name	**Number of engines**	**Country/ Region**
1)		*Beluga* _____	_____	_____
2)		_____ *Nasa Aero Space lines*	_____	_____
3)		_____ *Boeing*	_____	_____
4)		_____	_____	*Russia*
5)		*225* _____	_____	_____

8 Match these English proverbs with their meanings. Do you agree with them? Why or why not?

1) The cleanest journey is the one that does not take place.

2) The pilot who teaches himself has a fool for a student.

3) Everywhere is within walking distance if you have the time.

a ☐ If you are patient, you can always travel from one place to another.

b ☐ Every form of transport creates pollution in some way.

c ☐ It is impossible to learn to fly a plane without help from someone else.

9 The following table summarises the CO_2 emission factors by freight transport mode, established by Essen in 2003. Match transport modality with green tonality. Which is the greenest means of transport? Which is the most polluting one? Write a short paragraph to summarise these data.

	Modality	CO_2 emission g-t/km (expressed in grams CO_2 per tonne-kilometre)		
1)	Articulated lorry	60–80	A	
2)	Lorry 10–20 tonnes (local delivery)	120–150	B	
3)	Electric train	30–40	C	
4)	Diesel electric train	35–45	D	
5)	Ship 250–1,000 tonnes	35–70	E	
6)	Ship 1,000–3,000 tonnes	30–55	F	

CO_2 emission factors by freight transport mode (Essen et al., 2003)

Technical Terms

Boeing 747-400	波音747-400飞机
Antonov AN-225	安东诺夫-225运输机（为运输暴风雪号航天飞机而研制的超大型军用运输机）

UNIT 6 Handling Goods and Passengers

Learning Objectives

Upon completion of the unit, students will be able to:

- identify the organisation of warehouses, airports and ports;
- master the words and expressions related to storage areas and forklift truck;
- realise the importance of handling of goods and passengers properly.

Starting Off

1 **Write each means of handling goods and passengers under the picture.**

| forklift truck | loading bridge | airside transfer bus | pallet rack | crane | container |

1) _____

2) _____

3) _____

4) _____

5) _____

6) _____

Reading 1

Logistics and warehouses

A warehouse is a commercial building for storage of goods.

Warehouses are used by **manufacturers**, **importers**, **exporters**, **wholesalers**, transport businesses, etc. They are usually large **plain** buildings in **industrial** areas of cities, towns and villages, **strategically positioned** to be close to main transport facilities such as ports, roads, stations and rivers. They

usually have loading **docks** to load and unload goods from trucks. Sometimes warehouses are designed for the loading and unloading of goods directly from railways, airports, or seaports. They often have **cranes** and **forklift trucks** for moving goods, which are usually placed on ISO standard **pallets** loaded into pallet **racks**. **Stored** goods can include any raw materials, **packing** materials, **spare parts**, **components**, or **finished goods associated** with **agriculture**, **manufacturing**, or **commerce**.

Organising a warehouse well is essential for efficient loading, storing and unloading of goods, as it saves time, space and therefore money. Over the last twenty years warehouses have changed a lot, mainly due to new technology and business demands. Modern warehouses are now almost fully **automated**—they require very few people to run them—and they **employ** "Just in Time" techniques, so goods are never stored for very long, meaning savings in space and money.

MY GLOSSARY

manufacturer	*n.*	生产商, 厂家	rack	*n.*	架子, 搁物架
importer	*n.*	进口商; 进口国	store	*v.*	贮存, 贮藏
exporter	*n.*	出口商; 出口国	pack	*v.*	把……打包, 包装
wholesaler	*n.*	批发商	spare part		零部件
plain	*adj.*	普通的, 简单的	component	*n.*	组件; 组成部分
industrial	*adj.*	工业的, 产业的	finished goods		制成品, 成品
strategically	*adv.*	战略性地; 战略上	associate	*v.*	把……联系在一起
position	*v.*	安放, 放置	agriculture	*n.*	农业, 农艺
dock	*n.*	码头, 船坞	manufacture	*v.*	制造, 生产
crane	*n.*	吊车, 起重机	commerce	*n.*	商业, 贸易
forklift truck		叉车	automated	*adj.*	自动化的
pallet	*n.*	货板, 集装架	employ	*v.*	使用; 雇用

2 Read the text and answer the questions.

1) Why is the location of a warehouse so important?

2) What type of equipment is commonly used in a warehouse?

3) Why is the organisation of a warehouse so fundamental?

4) What factors have caused warehouses to change in recent years?

5) What are the consequences of automation in a warehouse?

3 **Match these words and phrases with their definitions.**

1) run   a ☐ planned for a particular purpose

2) pallet   b ☐ a small, low platform where goods are placed for storage

3) demands   c ☐ keeping in a particular place for future use

4) forklift truck   d ☐ a small vehicle with two front prongs for lifting and moving goods

5) strategical   e ☐ people who sell large quantities of goods for resale

6) wholesalers   f ☐ another word for "manage"

7) importers   g ☐ a machine for lifting and moving heavy weights

8) facilities   h ☐ another word for "requirements"

9) crane   i ☐ people who bring goods into a country to sell them

10) storing   j ☐ things designed to offer a particular service

Reading **2**

The term "logistics" is connected to the Greek word for **logic** and **rationale**, and it was first used with its **current** meaning of organisation in a **military context**. In the field of transportation logistics can be defined as "the **seamless** movement of goods from **supplier** to consumer, **accounting for** all the transport, handling and storage requirements in between". It includes operations such as exporting, **packaging**, marketing, **freight forwarding**, **consolidating**, **tracking**/monitoring, **clearance** and importing. As a result, freight logistics is a key **competitive** factor in business operations because it affects product quality, costs, profits, the ability to service customers and the ability to **retain** and **expand** market share.

MY GLOSSARY

logic	n.	逻辑, 逻辑学	package	v.	包装, 打包
rationale	n.	基本原理; 根本原因	freight forwarding		货运代理
current	adj.	当前的, 现在的	consolidate	v.	巩固, 加强
military	adj.	军事的; 军人的	tracking	n.	追踪, 跟踪
context	n.	环境; 语境	clearance	n.	清仓, 清理
seamless	adj.	无(接)缝的, 无空隙的	competitive	adj.	竞争的, 有竞争性的
supplier	n.	供应商, 供货商	retain	v.	保持, 保留
account for		(在数量上)占; 说明	expand	v.	扩大, 扩展

4 **Read the text and find the synonyms of the words below.**

1) managing _____

2) continuous _____

3) keep _____

4) increase _____

Reading 3

The forklift truck

A ☐ What is smaller than a car, stronger than an elephant, can reach as high as a giraffe, works like an **ox** and never falls over? The forklift truck! Everybody has a **vague** idea of the **existence** of this **humble** little machine, but very few people ever think about how it works and how important it is to us. Invented nearly a hundred years ago, the forklift truck is used in just about every industry—without it we would not be able to manufacture or transport goods the way we do.

B ☐ It was invented by a US company in 1917 for **internal** use, but quickly became popular with the company's **clients**, who wanted one for themselves. In 1930 the pallet was standardised, which led to a great increase in demand for the truck; and in the 1950s warehouses started to develop **vertically**—so the forklift followed in the same direction and was **redesigned** to be able to lift pallets to a height of 15 metres!

C ☐ There are in fact 7 different classes of forklift truck, mainly **differentiated** by their engines and **tyres**, but all forklifts share a series of common **characteristics**:
- **frame**, the **foundation** of all the forklift parts;
- **counterweight**, used to **stabilise** the forklift when lifting heavy loads;
- **mast**, **hydraulically** operated lift used to raise and lower a load;
- forks, **prongs** that lift up a wooden pallet;
- load **back-rest**, stops the load from **shifting** backwards;
- **overhead guard**, protects the operator from a falling load.

D ☐ The little truck has always been respected in industry for its **resistance** and **versatility**, but of course new technological progress has brought changes also to this machine: the 3 most significant of these are increased engine **efficiency**, making it more environmentally friendly; the arrival of the automated truck—controlled from a computer and no longer driven by an operator; and the "**sidewinder**" forklift, which can move in any direction, and so also to places that were **previously** off limits for this type of vehicle. It will certainly see more changes in the future too, but we can be sure that this little work horse will still be a common site in industry for years to come.

MY GLOSSARY

ox	n.	公牛, 牛
vague	adj.	模糊的, 含糊的
existence	n.	存在; 生存
humble	adj.	简陋的; 谦逊的
internal	adj.	内部的; 里面的
client	n.	客户; 委托人
vertically	adv.	垂直地, 直立地
redesign	v.	重新设计; 重新规划
differentiate	v.	区分, 区别
tyre	n.	轮胎
characteristic	n.	特性, 特色
frame	n.	框架, 结构
foundation	n.	基础; 地基
counterweight	n.	平衡重, 平衡锤

stabilise	v.	使稳定, 使坚固
mast	n.	杆, 桅杆
hydraulically	adv.	水压地
prong	n.	叉状物, 尖头
back-rest	n.	固定中心架, 靠背架
shift	v.	移动, 挪动
overhead guard		护顶架, 顶罩
resistance	n.	阻力; 抵抗
versatility	n.	多功能性, 通用性
efficiency	n.	效率, 效能
sidewinder	n.	响尾蛇
previously	adv.	以前, 预先

5 **Read the text and choose the best title for each paragraph (A–D).**

1) Recent changes

2) Features common to all trucks

3) Early development

4) Basic description of the forklift truck

6 **Read the text again and complete these sentences.**

1) Many more people wanted to use the forklift in the 1930s after _____.

2) The counterweight is fundamental for _____.

3) Protection for the operator is provided by _____.

4) The main characteristic of the automated truck is that _____.

5) The advantage of the "sidewinder" is that _____.

7 Find the synonyms of these words from the text.

1) unclear _____

2) make, assemble _____

3) remodeled _____

4) durability _____

Reading 4

The organisation of an airport

An airport is the **location** where aircraft take off and land, where goods, passengers and their **baggage transit**. Aircraft may be stored or maintained at an airport, where we usually **distinguish** two main parts: an **air side** and a **land side**. In the former we find all the infrastructures and services that serve to move aircraft, **runways**, **taxiways**, aircraft **parkings**, **aprons** and the air traffic control system; in the latter there are all the facilities and services associated with passengers such as the **access** to the airport, the terminal **footpaths** and the car parks. Gates are instead usually considered the border between the two areas.

The airport **ramp** or apron is the area where aircraft are parked, unloaded or loaded, refueled and boarded. The apron is not usually open to the general public and a **license** may be required to gain access.

The use of the apron may be controlled by the apron management service (apron control or apron advisory).

The apron is **designated** by the ICAO (International Civil Aviation Organisation) as not being part of the **maneuvering** area. All vehicles, aircraft and people using the apron **are referred to** as "apron traffic".

In the USA, the words "ramp" and "apron" are used **interchangeably** in most **circumstances**. Generally, the **preflight** activities are carried out on ramps and areas for parking and maintenance are called aprons.

location	*n.*	地点, 位置
baggage	*n.*	行李
transit	*n. / v.*	运输, 搬运
distinguish	*v.*	区分, 辨别
air side		机场周边活动区
land side		（对旅客开放的）机场公共场所
runway	*n.*	跑道, 滑道
taxiway	*n.*	（飞机的）滑行道
parking	*n.*	停车
apron	*n.*	停机坪
access	*n.*	通道, 进入

footpath	*n.*	人行道, 小径
ramp	*n.*	斜坡, 坡道; 活动舷梯
license	*n.*	执照, 许可证
designate	*v.*	指定, 划定（特征、用途）
maneuver	*v.*	演习; 机动
be referred to		被称作
interchangeably	*adv.*	可互换地, 可交换地
circumstance	*n.*	情况; 环境
preflight	*adj.*	起飞前的; 为起飞作准备的

8 Read the text and answer the questions.

1) What are the two most important parts we can distinguish in an airport?

2) To which of these parts do gates belong?

3) How can you define an apron?

4) Who controls the apron?

5) What does the acronym ICAO mean?

9 Match the apron vehicles' names with the correct definitions.

Each airport, according to its size and needs, has a different number and types of apron vehicles. There are however some basic ones which every airport must have and that you may have seen many times.

1) Follow Me

2) Push Back

3) Airside Transfer Bus (Apron Bus)

4) Loading Bridge (Jet Bridge)

a ☐ a movable staircase that passengers use to board or leave an aircraft

b ☐ a heavy tractor used to move aircraft from their parking spaces before taxing and taking off

c ☐ a cart used to carry passengers' baggage and goods to the aircraft before taking off and from them after landing

d ☐ They can be extra long and wide to hold the maximum number of passengers. They are usually fitted with minimal or no seating and with flashing beacons for operating

5) Baggage Dolly
(Pallet Dolly)

6) Passengers Boarding
Stairs

airside near runways. They may also have driving cabs at both ends.

e ☐ A ground vehicle, such as a jeep, that meets a landing airplane to lead it to its parking place. The words "follow me" usually appear on the rear of such vehicles.

f ☐ an enclosed, movable connector which extends from an airport terminal gate to an airplane, allowing passengers to board and disembark without having to go outside

Reading 5

The organisation of a port

A ☐ **Oslo** is **Norway**'s busiest ferry port with four daily **departures** to **Denmark** and Germany. The ferries carry over 2.6 million passengers a year and 1.2 million tons of freight. The freight carried by these ferries **constitutes** a third of the general cargo handled by the port of Oslo.

B ☐ Ferry traffic into and out of Oslo is expanding all the time with newer and ever larger ferries being taken into service.

C ☐ This **expansion** makes it imperative for the port to have efficient, **up to date** terminal buildings and also **adequate** space for vehicle ferry lines and for customer facilities for **disembarking** vehicles. Container transport is an expanding **segment** of the port of Oslo.

D ☐ The port currently has two container terminals, but development is **underway** to bring all container handling into one single terminal. When completed, this terminal will have a total **quay** length of 700 metres with a **minimum** water depth of 12 metres.

10 **Read the text and choose the best title for each paragraph (A–D).**

1) The trend in ferry traffic

2) General description of the port of Oslo

3) Future development

4) Key issues for the expansion of the port

11 **Find the synonyms of these words and phrases from the text.**

1) full of people and goods _____

2) managed _____

3) important _____

4) modern _____

5) growing _____

Listening

12 **Listen and complete the text with the correct words from the box.**

overseas	sheds	handling	shuttle	equipped	fuel	consumption	increase

The terminals are (1) _____ with two **gantry** cranes each. Container (2) _____ at the terminal is carried out by **straddle carriers** and RTG (rubber-tyred gantry) cranes. Most containers are (3) _____ cargo, but the volume of **short-sea** shipping containers is increasing. Forty-six thousand new cars are unloaded each year in the port of Oslo. There are two port (4) _____ for storage of new cars and unloading track for further distribution by rail with departures every day. The port of Oslo handles a large volume of **dry bulk**. An (5) _____ in construction work in the whole of Eastern Norway has resulted in heavy demand for **cement** and sand. The port has two quays for oil tankers. As much as forty percent of Norway's (6) _____ of oil products is unloaded at Oslo and stored in storage units. Air traffic in Eastern Norway is also dependent on the port of Oslo, which receives all the jet (7) _____ used at Oslo's Gardermoen airport. The fuel is then freighted to the airport by a daily rail (8) _____ .

MY GLOSSARY

gantry	n. 起重机龙门架, 门架	dry bulk	散装干货
straddle carrier	跨车, 跨运车	cement	n. 水泥
short-sea	n. 近海		

Technical Terms

ICAO (International Civil Aviation Organisation)　　国际民用航空组织

UNIT 7 Transport Documents

Learning Objectives

Upon completion of the unit, students will be able to:

- understand the significance of transport documents;
- master the words and expressions related to transport documents;
- distinguish different items in transport documents;
- complete or fill in a transport document with proper information.

Starting Off

1 Why do you think transport documents are necessary? What kind of information is indicated in them? Discuss in pairs.

Reading 1

Official transport **documents** must contain details and **instructions** relating to the transport and **consignment** of the goods. They usually show:

- the names of the **consignor** and **consignee**;
- the **point of origin** of the consignment and the **destination**;
- the route and method of **shipment**;
- the arrangements for the **payment** of freight.

Copies are generally kept by the consignor, consignee and **carrier**.

The road/rail consignment note

For road transport within the **EU**, the necessary document is called road **consignment note** or CMR and it **confirms** that the carrier has received the goods and that a **contract** of **carriage exists** between the **trader** and the carrier. For rail transport, the necessary document is called rail consignment note or CIM.

MY GLOSSARY					
document	*n.* 文件; 单据		consignee	*n.*	收货人
instruction	*n.* 指令, 指示		point of origin		起点
consignment	*n.* 托运; 托运的货物		destination	*n.*	目的地, 终点
consignor	*n.* 托运人		shipment	*n.*	装运, 运输

payment	*n.* 支付	contract	*n.* 合同, 契约
carrier	*n.* 承运人	carriage	*n.* 货运; 运费
EU	欧盟	exist	*v.* 存在; 生存
consignment note	托运单, 托运收据	trader	*n.* 交易商, 经商者
confirm	*v.* 确认, 确定		

2 Match the terms with the correct definitions.

1) consignor

2) consignee

3) destination

4) point of origin

5) insurance

a ☐ the place where someone is going or where something is being sent or taken

b ☐ a person or company that sends goods to someone, usually the person who is buying them

c ☐ an agreement in which you pay a company money and they pay your costs if you have an accident, injury, etc.

d ☐ the person something is sent to

e ☐ the place where something comes from

Reading 2

Focus on CMR

Seller: Hurlinton & Meads, 58 Grosvernor Square, Bristol, UK

Buyer: Hans Müller GmbH, Arabellastr. 92, Berlin, Germany

Goods: TV sets loaded on 10 pallets

Total gross weight: 2,010 kg

Carrier: TransEurope Express, 86 West Industrial Estate, Bristol

Registration plate No.: CV55PLO

Date of issue: 15th April 2020

Place of issue: Bristol

Annexed documents: Invoice No. 742

1 Sender (name, address, country)	INTERNATIONAL CONSIGNMENT NOTE
	JL 0054277
运输与物流英语	This carriage **is subject notwithstanding** any **clause** to the **contrary**, to the **Convention** on the Contract for the International Carriage of Goods by Road (CMR)

| 2 Consignee (name, address, country) | 16 Carrier (name, address, country) |

3 Place of **delivery** of the goods	17 **Successive** carriers (name, address, country)
Place	
Country	/

4 Place and date of taking over the goods	
Place	
Country	18 Carrier's **reservations** and **observations**
Date	
5 Annexed documents	/

6 Marks and Nos	7 Number of packages	8 Method of packing	9 Nature of the goods	10 Statistical number	11 Gross weight in kg	12 Volume in m³
/				/		/
UN Number	Official description	Warning **label**	Packing group			

13 Sender's instructions	19 To be paid by:	Sender	**Currency**	Consignee
	Carriage charges			
	Deductions			
/ (CMR)	**Balance**			
	Supplementary charges		/	
	Other charges			
	Others			
	Total			

14 **Reimbursement**

15 Instructions as to payment for carriage	20 Special agreements
Carriage paid	/
Carriage forward	
Established in /	Date	23 Goods received	Date

| 21 **Signature** and stamp of the sender | 22 Signature and stamp of the carrier | Signature and stamp of the consignee |
| / | / | / |
| 24 Registration plate number |

registration plate No.		注册车牌号	clause	n.	条款
date of issue		签发日期, 出票日期	contrary	n.	相反, 反面
place of issue		签发地点		adj.	相反的
annexed	adj.	附加的	convention	n.	公约
invoice	n.	发票	successive	adj.	连续的
delivery	n.	交付, 交货	reservation	n.	保留, 预订
nature	n.	性质	observation	n.	观察; 观察报告
statistical	adj.	统计的; 统计学的	currency	n.	货币, 现金; 通货
label	n.	标签, 标记	deduction	n.	扣除, 减除
reimbursement	n.	赔偿	balance	n.	余额
be subject to		服从; 依据	supplementary charge		额外费用
notwithstanding	adv.	尽管, 虽然	signature	n.	签名, 签字

3 Complete the CMR with the information provided in Reading 2.

Reading 3

The bill of lading

The bill of lading (B/L) is the document used for sea freight and it serves as a **document of title**, a contract of carriage and a **receipt** of goods. As a receipt, it **states** the condition of the goods when they are loaded on the ship. As a document of title, it enables the consignee to receive, retain, sell or otherwise **dispose of** the document and goods by **endorsing** it to a new consignee. There are two types of bill of lading:

- a clean B/L: the carrier declares the goods have been received **on board** in **apparent** good order and condition;
- a foul B/L: the carrier declares the goods (or packaging) looked in **unsatisfactory** condition when loaded on board.

TRANSBRAZ
SHIPPING LINE

ORIGINAL

BILL OF LADING
FOR MULTIMODAL TRANSPORT
AND PORT TO PORT SHIPMENT

SHIPPER/EXPORTER (COMPLETE NAME/STREET ADDRESS) Coffee Export sa Rva Pedro Alves 270 Santos, Sao Paulo, Brazil	MANIFEST NO.	BILL OF LADING NO. TBSL 0042
	EXPORT REFERENCES	

CONSIGNEE (NOT NEGOTIABLE UNLESS CONSIGNED 'TO ORDER') To order	FORWARDING AGENT REFERENCES
	POINT AND COUNTRY OF ORIGIN

NOTIFY PARTY (COMPLETE NAME/STREET ADDRESS) C. J. Parker & Sons 265 Main Street 27047 Greensboro, NC, USA	ALSO NOTIFY, ROUTING & INSTRUCTIONS

PRE-CARRIAGE BY (MODE) *	PLACE OF RECEIPT *	FOR DELIVERY OF GOODS PLEASE APPLY TO 27047 Greensboro forwarding 594 Livingston Road 27409 Greensboro, NC, USA Phone (336)852-5484 Fax (336)852-5490
OCEAN VESSEL/VOYAGE Sea Lion/V050N	PORT OF LOADING Santos, Brazil	
PORT OF DISCHARGE Norfolk, VA, USA	PLACE OF DELIVERY * Norfolk, VA, USA	

PARTICULARS DECLARED BY SHIPPER

MARKS AND NUMBERS CONTAINER AND SEAL NUMBERS	PURCHASE ORDER NUMBER/ITEM NUMBER	NUMBER AND DESCRIPTION OF PACKAGES AND GOODS	GROSS WEIGHT
THCU7425658/986475/40' CE0589 P/NO. 1-20		1 (ONE) X 40' CONTAINER SAID TO CONTAIN 20 PALLETS - BAGS OF WHITE REFINED SUGAR FREIGHT COLLECT	20,000 KGS

FREIGHT/CHARGES, ITEM NO. RAE/RATE BASIS	PREPAID	COLLECT As arranged	EXCESS VALUE DECLARATION REFER TO CLAUSE 6 (4) (B) + (C) ON REVERSE SIDE
			RECEIVED BY THE CARRIER IN APPARENT GOOD ORDER AND CONDITION UNLESS OTHERWISE STATED FOR CARRIAGE BY OCEAN VESSEL AND/OR OTHER MODES OF TRANSPORT FROM THE PLACE OF RECEIPT OR PORT OF LOADING TO THE PORT OF DISCHARGE OR PLACE OF DELIVERY AS INDICATED ABOVE. GOODS TO BE DELIVERED AT THE ABOVE MENTIONED PORT OF DISCHARGE OR PLACE OF DELIVERY WHICHEVER APPLIES. IN ACCEPTING THIS BILL OF LADING THE SHIPPER(S) AGREE TO BE BOUND BY ALL STIPULATIONS, EXCEPTION, TERMS AND CONDITIONS ON THE FRONT OR BACK THEREOF, WHETHER PRINTED, STAMPED, WRITTEN OR OTHERWISE INCORPORATED. IN WITNESS WHEREOF THREE ORIGINAL BILLS OF LADING HAVE BEEN SIGNED, IF NOT OTHERWISE STATED ABOVE ONE ORIGINAL BILL OF LADING DULY ENDORSED MUST BE SURRENDERED IN EXCHANGE FOR THE GOODS, UPON WHICH THE OTHER(S) SHALL STAND VOID
FREIGHT PAYABLE AT Destination	TOTAL FREIGHT		
NUMBER OF ORIGINAL BILLS OF LADING Three (3)	PLACE AND DATE OF ISSUE Santos, 12.18.2020		
LADEN ON BOARD DATE 12.18.2020		*Ricardo Coelho*	
*APPLICABLE ONLY WHEN USED AS A MULTIMODAL TRANSPORT DOCUMENT. INSOFAR AS THIS BILL OF LADING IS ISSUED AS A MULTIMODAL TRANSPORT DOCUMENT IT IS BASED ON THE I.C.C. UNIFORM RULES FOR A MULTIMODAL TRANSPORT DOCUMENT I.C.C. PUBLICATION NO. 48	SIGNED AS AGENT FOR THE CARRIER: Transbraz Shipping Line		

document of title		物权凭证	notify party		到货受通知方, 被通知人
receipt	n.	收据, 收条	vessel	n.	船舶
state	v.	规定; 声明; 陈述	voyage	n.	航程
dispose of		处理, 解决	port of discharge		卸货港
endorse	v.	背书	item	n.	物品; 条款
on board		已装船, 在船上	rate basis		费率基础
apparent	adj.	清晰可见的; 显而易见的	laden	v.	装载, 负载
unsatisfactory	adj.	不能令人满意的	forwarding agent		货运代理人
negotiable	adj.	可转让的; 可协商的			

4 **Look at the B/L in Reading 3 and answer these questions.**

1) Who is the consignor?

2) Which port are the goods being shipped from?

3) Which port will they be delivered to?

4) What is the name of the ship?

5) What goods are being shipped?

6) How are they packed?

7) How much do they weigh?

8) When were they loaded on board?

  # Reading 4

The air waybill

The air **waybill** (AWB) is the document used when transporting freight by air.

It serves as a receipt of goods by the airline and as a contract of carriage. It is non-negotiable. It includes a description of the goods, instructions, conditions of carriage, **limitations** of **liability** and **applicable** transportation charges.

Consignor's Name and Address	Shipper's account Number	Not negotiable **Air Waybill**	
ABC Co 1-8-1 Nihonbashi Chuo Ku Tokyo Japan		issued by ALL NIPPON AIRWAYS CO., LTD Shiodome City Center 1-5-2, Higashi-Shimbashi, Minato-ku, Tokyo 105-7133, JAPAN	**ANA** All Nippon Airways

Copies 1,2 and 3 of this Air Waybill are originals and have the same validity

Consignee's Name and Address	Consignee's account Number
Grayson Co 1566 Cassil Place Los Angeles CA 90028	

It is agreed that the goods described herein are accepted in apparent good order and condition (except as noted) for carriage SUBJECT TO THE CONDITIONS OF CONTRACT ON THE REVERSE HEREOF. ALL GOODS MAY BE CARRIED BY ANY OTHER MEANS INCLUDING ROAD OR ANY OTHER CARRIER UNLESS SPECIFIC CONTRARY INSTRUCTIONS ARE GIVEN HEREON BY THE SHIPPER, AND SHIPPER AGREES THAT THE SHIPMENT MAY BE CARRIED VIA INTERMEDIATE STOPPING PLACES WHICH THE CARRIER DEEMS APPROPRIATE. THE SHIPPER'S ATTENTION IS DRAWN TO THE NOTICE CONCERNING CARRIER'S LIMITATION OF LIABILITY. Shipper may increase such limitation of liability by declaring a higher value for carriage and paying a supplemental charge if required.

Issuing Carrier's Agent Name and City	Accounting Information
	PRIO EXPRESS

Agent's IATA Code	Account No.

Airport of Departure (Addr. of first Carrier) and requested Routing	Reference Number	Optional Shipping Information
NARITA		

to	By first Carrier Routing and Destination	to	by	to	by	Currency	CHGS Code	WT/VAL PPD COLL	Other PPD COLL	Declared Value for Carriage	Declared Value for Customs
	NH006/01OCT2008										

Airport of Destination	Flight/Date	For Carrier Use only	Flight/Date	Amount of Insurance	INSURANCE - If carrier offers insurance, and such insurance is requested in accordance with the conditions thereof, indicate amount to be insured in figures in box marked 'amount of insurance'
Los Angeles				0	

Handling Information

FAX: 340-123-4568   Contact Person: Mr. John Knowles

SCI

No. of Pieces RCP	Gross Weight	kg lb	Rate Class / Commodity Item No.	Chargeable Weight	Rate / Charge	Total	Nature and Quantity of Goods (Incl. Dimensions or Volume)
1	5.0	k	M	5.0	14,000	14,000	IC PARTS
1	5.0					14,000	

Prepaid	Weight Charge	Collect	Other Charges
USD 14,000			

Valuation Charge

Tax

Total other Charges Due Agent

Shipper certifies that the particulars on the face hereof are correct and that insofar as any part of the consignment contains dangerous goods, such part is properly described by name and is in proper condition for carriage by air according to the applicable Dangerous Goods Regulations.

Total other Charges Due Carrier

Signature of Shipper or his Agent

Total prepaid	Total collect
USD 14,000	

Currency Conversion Rates	cc charges in Dest. Currency

Executed on   (Date)   at   (Place)   Signature of issuing Carrier or its Agent

For Carrier's Use only at Destination	Charges at Destination	Total collect Charges

MY GLOSSARY

waybill	*n.*	运单, 货运单	
limitation	*n.*	限制, 局限	
liability	*n.*	责任; 债务	

applicable	*adj.*	适用的, 适合的

5 **Look at the AWB in Reading 4 and find the following information.**

1) name of the airline _____

2) consignor _____

3) consignee _____

4) goods (type, size, weight, quantity) _____

5) point of origin _____

6) destination _____

7) insurance _____

8) total value _____

Speaking

6 **Prepare a short presentation (3–5 minutes) about international transport documents, explaining which documents are needed and the information they contain.**

Technical Terms

road consignment note (CMR)	公路托运单
rail consignment note (CIM)	铁路托运单
bill of lading (B/L)	提单
clean B/L	清洁提单, 不附带条件的提单
foul B/L	不清洁提单, 有不良批注提单
air waybill (AWB)	空运提单

UNIT
8 Insurance

Learning Objectives

Upon completion of the unit, students will be able to:

• understand the significance of insurance in transport;

• master the words and expressions related to insurance;

• recognise different categories of marine and business insurance.

Starting Off

1 **Listen and answer the questions.**

1) What was the man calling for?

2) Who was the shipping agent?

3) Where were the goods shipped from?

4) When did the ship arrive?

5) What was the reference number?

Reading 1

Insurance

Insurance is the way in which people and businesses protect themselves against risks.

In the UK and many other countries, some kinds of insurance are **compulsory** for individuals, like **motor** insurance for driving a car or buildings insurance if you have a **mortgage** on your home. Other kinds of insurance, such as protection against theft, accident or illness, are **optional**. **Similarly**, for business there are compulsory and optional insurances. Compulsory insurances are **employer**'s liability insurance and motor insurance, while optional ones include protection against theft, damages, fire, etc. The insurance policy has to be **renewed periodically**, normally every year. If a **policyholder** makes a **valid claim**, the **insurer** will **pay out** the amount of **compensation** agreed.

MY GLOSSARY

insurance	*n.*	保险; 保险业	periodically	*adv.*	定期地, 周期性地
compulsory	*adj.*	强制的, 必须做的			
motor	*n.*	机动车	policyholder	*n.*	投保人, 保单持有人
mortgage	*n.*	按揭, 抵押贷款	valid	*adj.*	有效的; 正式认可的
optional	*adj.*	可选择的	claim	*n.*	索赔; 声称
similarly	*adv.*	同样地; 相似地	insurer	*n.*	承保人; 保险公司
employer	*n.*	雇主, 老板	pay out		支付, 付出
renew	*v.*	延长……的期限; 更新	compensation	*n.*	赔偿金, 补偿金

2 Read the text and decide if these sentences are true (*T*) or false (*F*). If there is not enough information, choose "doesn't say" (*DS*).

	T	F	DS
1) Insurance is a kind of financial protection for both individuals and businesses.	☐	☐	☐
2) A driver must have motor insurance for his/her car.	☐	☐	☐
3) A company is not obliged to have any kind of insurance.	☐	☐	☐
4) Insurance brokers work for insurance companies.	☐	☐	☐
5) Insurance premiums increase annually.	☐	☐	☐
6) It is necessary to renew insurance policies.	☐	☐	☐

3 Match each word with the correct definition.

1) premium	a	☐	the money awarded to a victim of loss/damage by an insurance company
2) policyholder	b	☐	a demand for money under the conditions of an insurance policy
3) underwrite	c	☐	the amount of money to be paid for an insurance contract
4) insurer	d	☐	the person or company who offers advice and sells insurance
5) claim	e	☐	to sign and accept liability
6) compensation	f	☐	the person/business in whose name the insurance contract is held

Reading 2

Focus on marine insurance

Marine insurance is one of the oldest forms of insurance. Exporters and importers doing international business need to **organise** their own marine insurance against the risks of loss or damage to their goods in transit. There are many different policies, with **varying** conditions and **exclusions**, but the **principal** forms are:

- voyage policy is an insurance **cover** for one **particular** voyage;
- time policy is valid for a specified time period;
- valued policy is the one where the value of the cargo and consignment is **indicated**, so the amount of any compensation is known **in advance**;
- unvalued policy is the one where the value of the cargo and consignment are not indicated, so the amount of compensation will be agreed after;
- floating policy is the one where a total insured amount is specified and the details of the ship, voyage, etc. are declared at the moment of departure. This is the most common open policy for frequent shipments.

organise	*v.*	安排, 组织	cover	*n.*	（保险）范围
varying	*adj.*	变化多端的, 多种多样的		*v.*	投保; 包含
			particular	*adj.*	特定的, 具体的
exclusion	*n.*	除外责任; 排除	indicate	*v.*	表明, 指出
principal	*adj.*	主要的, 最重要的	in advance		预先, 提前

Reading 3

Business insurance

As mentioned previously, there are two types of compulsory insurance for businesses in the UK:

- Employers' liability insurance. This **insures** all company employees against **injury**, disease or death as a result of their **employment**, workplace conditions or practices.

- Motor insurance. This is compulsory if the company owns and operates any kind of vehicle on public roads. However, no modern business would operate **solely** with compulsory insurance. If something went wrong—a fire in a **production plant**, the theft of goods, injury to a customer—it would cost the company a great deal of money and it could even force them out of business. Therefore it is normal to **take out** insurance policies to cover further risks and liabilities. The different kinds of business insurance can be divided into three main areas:

Protection against loss or damage

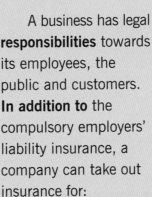

It is important for a company to protect both its property and its trade from damage and loss, so there are many policies for this area, including:

- buildings and contents insurance against fire, **lightning**, **explosion**, **floods**, etc;
- cover against electrical and mechanical **breakdown** of machinery, including computers;
- contents insurance against theft, which can also include a money policy to cover cash, cheques, **postage stamps** and other negotiable documents;
- insurance of goods in transit;
- cover against business **interruption** and loss of income;
- **trade credit** cover, which may be particularly important for exporters and covers bad **debt** due to **default** and **insolvency**;
- legal **expenses** insurance.

Protection against legal liabilities to third parties

A business has legal **responsibilities** towards its employees, the public and customers. **In addition to** the compulsory employers' liability insurance, a company can take out insurance for:

- public liability which covers its legal liabilities for death or injury to people and damage to property **arising from** its business activities;
- product liability which covers damage or injury arising from **defects** in product design and manufacture.

Personal protection for owners and employees

The **temporary** or **permanent** loss of a key person in a business — due to illness, injury or death — can have a significant effect on a business, so there are policies which can help reduce this impact. These include:

- personal accident and sickness insurance, particularly important for small companies and the **self-employed**;
- income protection insurance;
- private **medical** insurance;
- life insurance and **pensions**.

MY GLOSSARY

insure	v.	投保, 给……上保险	plant	n.	工厂; 植物
injury	n.	伤害, 损害	take out		办理; 取出
employment	n.	工作, 职业	lightning	n.	闪电
solely	adv.	仅, 只; 唯一地	explosion	n.	爆炸
production	n.	生产; 制造	flood	n.	洪水, 水灾

breakdown	*n.*	故障; 崩溃		in addition to		除……之外
postage stamp		邮票		arise from		由……引起, 起因于
interruption	*n.*	中断; 干扰		defect	*n.*	缺陷, 缺点
trade credit		商业信用		temporary	*adj.*	暂时的, 临时的
debt	*n.*	债务, 欠债		permanent	*adj.*	永久的, 长久的
default	*n.*	违约, 拖欠		self-employed	*adj.*	自雇的; 自由职业的
insolvency	*n.*	破产, 无力偿还		medical	*adj.*	医疗的, 医学的
expense	*n.*	费用, 开销		pension	*n.*	养老金, 退休金
responsibility	*n.*	责任, 职责				

4 Read the text and answer these questions.

1) What types of insurance are compulsory for businesses?

2) How can equipment and machinery be insured?

3) Is it possible to insure cash?

4) What is trade credit insurance?

5) Why are product and public liability insurance so important?

6) What personal insurance is important if you work for yourself? Why?

Reading 4

Focus on Lloyd's

The story of Lloyd's began in a small coffee house in the City of London in 1688. Edward Lloyd's coffee house was a favourite meeting place for ships' captains, **merchants** and **shipowners** and it had a **reputation** for trustworthy shipping news. Then, as London's importance as a trade centre grew, it became recognised as the place for obtaining marine insurance. From those **modest** beginnings, Lloyd's has been a **pioneer** in insurance and has grown over 300 years to become the world's leading insurance market. Lloyd's, in fact, is not an insurance company which directly sells insurance, but an insurance

Lloyd's building was designed by the architect Richard Rogers and took eight years to build.

market where its members can meet potential clients and join together as **syndicates** to insure risk. The risks Lloyd's covers can be **grouped** into 7 main categories: **casualty**, property, marine, energy, motor, aviation and **reinsurance**. Reinsurance is when an insurance company, in order to lower its own risks and potential financial losses, transfers part of its **portfolio** of risks to other parties. Lloyd's is made by the Market and the Corporation of Lloyd's.

The Market **structure** encourages innovation, speed and better value, making it attractive to policyholders and **participants alike**. The Corporation **oversees** and supports the Market and **promotes** Lloyd's around the world.

MY GLOSSARY

merchant	*n.*	商人, 批发商			战争中的）伤亡人员
shipowner	*n.*	船主			
reputation	*n.*	声望, 名誉	reinsurance	*n.*	再保险; 分保
modest	*adj.*	（数量、比率或改进幅度等）较小的; 适度的, 适中的	portfolio	*n.*	投资组合
			structure	*n.*	结构, 构造
			participant	*n.*	参与者, 参加者
pioneer	*n.*	开拓者, 先锋	alike	*adv.*	相似地, 类似地
syndicate	*n.*	辛迪加; 企业联合组织	oversee	*v.*	监督, 审查
group	*v.*	把……分组	promote	*v.*	促进; 促销
casualty	*n.*	意外事故;（严重事故或			

5 **Read the text and decide if these sentences are true (*T*) or false (*F*). If there is not enough information, choose "doesn't say" (*DS*).**

	T	F	DS
1) Lloyd's is the leading insurance company in the world.	☐	☐	☐
2) Edward Lloyd was the creator of marine insurance.	☐	☐	☐
3) The Market and Lloyd's Corporation have two separate roles.	☐	☐	☐
4) Coverholders specialise in certain categories of risk.	☐	☐	☐
5) The market structure keeps fixed and stable for many years, which makes it attractive.	☐	☐	☐

Writing

6 Find out about an important event in the history of Lloyd's (e.g. The Titanic, the 1906 San Francisco earthquake). Write a report on what happened, how Lloyd's was involved, the insurance premiums and claims, etc.

Speaking

7 Discuss with your partner about business insurance in China.

Technical Terms

motor insurance	机动车保险
employer's liability insurance	雇主责任保险
marine insurance	海上保险
voyage policy	航程保单
time policy	定期保单
valued policy	定值保单
unvalued policy	不定值保单
floating policy	流动保单
contents insurance	家庭财产保险
life insurance	人寿保险

Learning Objectives

Upon completion of the unit, students will be able to:

• realise the importance of safety procedures and regulations;

• master the words and expressions related to safety procedures and regulations;

• raise the awareness of following safety procedures and regulations at work and in transport.

Starting Off

1 **Write the translation of the following words and expressions in Chinese. Then read the text to learn more about safety legislation.**

1) danger　　　_____

2) workplace　_____

3) guidelines　_____

4) assessment　_____

5) employer　　_____

6) worker　　　_____

7) act　　　　_____

8) workstation　_____

9) clothing　　_____

10) equipment　_____

11) first aid　　_____

12) insurance　_____

Reading 1

Safety regulations and legislation

In the field of transport and logistics, like in all areas of work, safety is a fundamental consideration. In all workplaces today there are **guidelines** to follow in order to avoid accidents, which explain what risks exist at work, their potential danger, and how to avoid them. Employers **are obliged to inform** their workers of these **indications**. The following is **authentic** information from European **legislation**:

- Employers' Liability (Compulsory Insurance) Act 1969: this act requires employers to take out insurance against accidents and ill health to their employees.
- Health and Safety (**First Aid**) Regulations 1981: they cover requirements for first aid.
- Health and Safety Information for Employees Regulations 1989: they require employers to **display** a **poster** telling employees what they need to know about health and safety.
- Workplace Regulations 1992: they cover a wide range of basic health and safety issues such as **ventilation**, **heating**, **lighting**, **workstations**, **seating** and facilities.
- Personal Protective Equipment at Work Regulations 1992: they require employers to provide **appropriate protective** clothing and **equipment** for their employees.
- Reporting of Injuries, Diseases and Dangerous **Occurrences** Regulations 1995 (RIDDOR): they require employers to **notify** certain **occupational** injuries, diseases and dangerous events.
- **Provision** and Use of Work Equipment Regulations 1998: they require that equipment provided for use at work, including machinery, is safe.
- Management of Health and Safety at Work Regulations 1999: they require employers to carry out risk **assessments** and arrange for appropriate information and training.
- Control of Substances **Hazardous** to Health Regulations 2002 (COSHH): they require employers to **assess** the risks from hazardous **substances** and take appropriate **precautions**.

guideline	n.	准则; 指导方针
be obliged to		有义务, 不得不
inform	v.	通知, 告知
indication	n.	指示, 标示
authentic	adj.	真的, 真正的
legislation	n.	立法, 法规
first aid		急救
display	v.	展示, 陈列
poster	n.	海报; 广告
ventilation	n.	通风, 通风设备
heating	n.	暖气, 采暖
lighting	n.	照明, 采光
workstation	n.	工作区, 工作站

seating	n.	座次, 座位
appropriate	adj.	适当的, 恰当的
protective	adj.	防护的, 保护的
equipment	n.	设备, 装备
occurrence	n.	发生, 出现
notify	v.	通报, 通知
occupational	adj.	职业的
provision	n.	规定, 条款
assessment	n.	评估; 估价
hazardous	adj.	危险的; 有害的
assess	v.	评估; 估价
substance	n.	物质
precaution	n.	预防措施, 预防

2 Read the text and answer the questions.

1) Is it obligatory for employers to insure their staff against injury?

2) Which regulations are concerned with first aid?

3) Which regulations deal with the environment in the workplace?

4) Who is responsible for protective clothing in the workplace?

5) What action must employers take in case of injuries?

6) What did the 1999 work regulations introduce?

3 Find synonyms of these words and phrases from the text.

1) important _____

2) workers _____

3) variety _____

4) suitable _____

5) declare _____

6) given _____

7) free from danger _____

8) organise _____

9) dangerous _____

4 Look at the picture. Have you ever seen these signs? Do you know their meanings? What do you have to do when they are lit during a flight? Tick the correct answers.

1) ☐ You mustn't use your mobile phone.

2) ☐ You mustn't smoke.

3) ☐ You can remain seated or stand up.

4) ☐ You must remain seated and fasten your seatbelt.

Reading 2

5 In pairs, look at the picture and answer the questions. Then read the text and check your knowledge about safety regulations.

1) What do these new restrictions concern?

2) Are they valid for all flights?

3) What is the maximum quantity of liquids you can take in your hand luggage?

4) Where do you have to put liquids?

5) Can you take a 200 ml sun cream in your hand luggage? Why or why not?

New regulations for hand luggage

There are **restrictions** on liquids which can be taken into the cabin on flights **originating** within the EU.

- ► Volume max. 1 l
- ► Re-sealable
- ► Transparent

max. 100 ml

max. 100 ml

Please present separately at the Security Control.

Safety regulations for air passengers

If you have travelled by airplane, you will know that there are many safety procedures to follow before and during your journey. When you arrive at the airport, your **identity** is checked several times, and you have to pass through security **checkpoints**. When you are on the plane and ready for take-off, you have to listen to the in-flight safety procedures to understand what to do in case of an emergency. When you arrive at your destination, your identity may be checked again and you may be asked to open your bags for **inspection**. If you are carrying liquids in your hand luggage, for example, they may be taken away from you. But why are all these safety checks so important? The main reason is to prevent acts of **terrorism**. Many liquids, such as **perfume** and aerosols, can be used to create **explosives**; computers can be **programmed** to control explosive **devices**; and many metal objects may be used as weapons — so controlling these items is fundamental to guarantee the safety of all passengers.

MY GLOSSARY

hand luggage		手提行李
restriction	*n.*	限制, 约束
originate	*v.*	起源, 发生
identity	*n.*	身份
checkpoint	*n.*	检查站, 关卡
inspection	*n.*	检查, 查看

terrorism	*n.*	恐怖行为, 恐怖主义
perfume	*n.*	香水
explosive	*n.* *adj.*	炸药, 爆炸物 爆炸性的
programme	*v.*	编程
device	*n.*	装置, 器械

Reading 3

Air safety

Many people feel very frightened when they travel by plane, but you may not know that, in fact, air travel is **statistically** the safest form of **motorised** transport known to man! Today it is **estimated** that there is only one **fatality** for every 2,000 million person-miles flown in the air. Accurate communication between the pilot and the ground is obviously fundamental for air safety, and indeed many accidents are caused when this information is inaccurate or provided too late. Four out of five accidents occur during take-off or landing procedures, that's why you must always seat with your **seatbelt fastened** during these procedures and you are not allowed to use electronic devices.

Another cause of accidents could be the **presence** of ice or snow on the wings, which increases the weight of the plane, requiring a higher speed to avoid **stalling**. Engine failure rarely causes accidents in large aircraft because they operate with several engines, so an emergency landing is usually possible.

When an airplane flies through **volcanic** ash, its engines can lose power completely. Today, **meteorological** information is so precise that **airspace** is simply closed in the presence of volcanic ash, as in the case of the **eruptions** in Iceland in 2010.

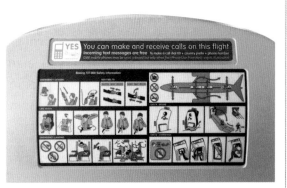

Aircraft safety is improving all the time. However it is important to read carefully and know all the safety indications on the passenger safety card.

MY GLOSSARY

statistically	*adv.*	统计地; 统计学上地		presence	*n.*	出现, 存在
motorised	*adj.*	机动的, 机动化的		stall	*v.*	(使)(发动机)熄火
estimate	*v.*	估计; 估价		volcanic	*adj.*	火山的; 火山引起的
fatality	*n.*	死亡		meteorological	*adj.*	气象的; 气象学的
seatbelt	*n.*	安全带		airspace	*n.*	(某国的)空域, 领空
fasten	*v.*	系牢, 扣紧		eruption	*n.*	喷发, 爆发

6 **Read the text and decide if these statements are true (*T*) or false (*F*).**

	T	F
1) Only one person in 2,000 million die in an air crash.	☐	☐
2) 80% of air accidents occur on or near the ground.	☐	☐
3) Many accidents are the result of poor communication.	☐	☐
4) Each airplane accident helps in research to improve safety.	☐	☐

Reading 4

Road safety

Road safety is something that concerns everyone, because we all use roads in some way—not everyone drives their own means of transport, but most of us use public transport and everybody has to cross the road of course!

Of all the areas of human activity where safety is a concern, the field of road transport is probably the most important. Road accidents are one of the most common **causes** of **accidental** death in the world, with an estimated 1 million people dying in road-related accidents every year, so it is **logical** that a lot of time and money are spent on constantly improving road safety across the planet. Great developments in this field have been **achieved** in recent times, **in particular with regard to** the safety of vehicles and roads themselves—just consider the **airbag**, ABS **braking**, improved road **layouts**, **speed bumps**, cat's eyes, better **signposting**, **draining asphalt** and in very recent times the introduction of **sobriety** devices—which drivers have to breathe into before they can start a vehicle. Today the focus is shifting to the **pedestrian**, after statistics have shown that the **majority** of **victims** of road accidents are people on foot or on bicycles. The use of **cycling lanes**, **underpasses** for pedestrians and reduced speed limits in urban areas are just a few examples of how greater attention is now being paid to improving the safety of people on foot or non-motorised transport.

MY GLOSSARY

cause	*n.*	原因, 起因
accidental	*adj.*	意外的; 偶然的
logical	*adj.*	合理的, 符合逻辑的
achieve	*v.*	达到, 取得
in particular		尤其, 特别
with regard to		关于, 至于
airbag	*n.*	安全气囊
brake	*v.*	刹车, 制动
layout	*n.*	布局; 设计

speed bump		减速带
signpost	*v.*	设置路标
draining asphalt		沥青路面
sobriety	*n.*	未醉, 清醒
pedestrian	*n.*	行人, 步行者
majority	*n.*	大部分, 大多数
victim	*n.*	受害者, 罹难者
cycling lane		自行车车道
underpass	*n.*	地下通道

7 Read the text and complete the sentences.

1) Road safety is one of the most important areas of _____.

2) A lot of people die every year because of _____.

3) Great developments have helped improving road safety, for example new cars equipped with airbag and _____.

4) Today most victims of road accidents are pedestrians or _____.

8 Here are a series of common road signs. Match them to their meanings.

1) ☐ parking

2) ☐ yield

3) ☐ intersection

4) ☐ double curve

5) ☐ pedestrian crossing

6) ☐ uneven road

7) ☐ school crossing

8) ☐ passing prohibited

9) ☐ no entry

10) ☐ no parking

11) ☐ no vehicle traffic

12) ☐ traffic lights ahead

A

B

C

D

9 **Complete the table by putting the safety features from the box in the right column.**

| seat belts | road signs | cycling lanes | speed bumps | guardrails | brake lights | underpasses |
| pedestrian crossings | ABS | speed cameras | airbags | cycling helmets |

On vehicles	Features for users	Infrastructures
seat belts		

Reading 5

Fleet monitoring

One **controversial scheme** for improving an aspect of road safety has been the introduction of the so-called "**fleet monitoring**". You may have seen lorries, vans and other commercial vehicles driving on the streets with a sign printed on them similar to the one above. This sign is an invitation for the general public to inform transport companies of any improper behaviour by their drivers. If you see a vehicle driving too fast, **overtaking** dangerously or not respecting signals or limits, then you can call the number on the sign to report the incident. This invitation to make the normal **citizen** responsible has proven to be very useful to transport companies who have to pay large insurance premiums and feel the need to make sure that their drivers are behaving correctly and efficiently at all times. Of course, the scheme has been **criticised** by many people, as they feel that it can be **abused**—some people have reported drivers simply because they had an argument with them, for example; and others feel that it also encourages a form of **spying**. Whatever you think the "fleet monitoring" scheme is certainly popular with employers in the field, so it appears destined to grow.

MY GLOSSARY

controversial	adj.	有争议的, 引起争论的	criticise	v.	批评, 批判
scheme	n.	计划, 方案	abuse	v.	滥用, 妄用
fleet monitoring		车队监控	spy	v.	从事间谍活动; 搜集情报
overtake	v.	超车, 赶上			
citizen	n.	公民, 居民			

10 Read the text and answer the questions.

1) What is the "fleet monitoring" scheme?

2) Why was it introduced?

3) When should the public use the telephone number?

4) Why has the scheme been criticised by some people?

5) Is there anything similar in China? What is your opinion of it, and why?

11 Here are some common railway signs. Match the signs to their meanings. Then read the text to learn more about railroad safety.

1) railroad crossing

2) St Andrew Cross: stop and check for an approaching train

3) danger: high voltage

4) don't cross the tracks

5) step over the gap when getting on and off a train

NO STEPPING OVER

Railroad safety focuses on six main safety **disciplines** which include:

- hazardous materials;
- equipment;
- operating practices (including **drug** and **alcohol** abuse);
- signal and train control;
- tracks;
- rail and infrastructure **integrity**.

In Great Britain The Railway Safety Regulations were introduced in 1999. These regulations require a compulsory protection system both for the trains and railways and new safety measures for passengers and workers as well.

MY GLOSSARY

discipline	*n.* 纪律; 约束	alcohol	*n.* 酒精
drug	*n.* 毒品	integrity	*n.* 完整, 完好

Reading 6

The European Maritime Safety Agency (EMSA), based in Lisbon, provides support to the **European Commission** in the development of EU legislation on **maritime** safety, pollution by ships and maritime security.

EMSA was set up in 2003 after two major accidents at sea: the Erika (1999) and the Prestige (2002) accidents and their resulting oil spills. These incidents resulted in huge environmental and economic damage to the **coastlines** of Spain and France.

EMSA's main **objective** is to reduce the risk of maritime accidents, marine pollution from ships and the loss of human life at sea.

MY GLOSSARY

European Commission	欧盟委员会	coastline	n.	海岸线
maritime	adj. 海的; 海事的	objective	n.	目标, 目的

12 **Read the text and answer the questions.**

1) Where is EMSA's headquarters?

2) When was it created?

3) Which two European countries were damaged by the Erika and Prestige accidents?

4) What are the main tasks EMSA has to accomplish?

Listening

13 **Listen to an expert talking about IMO and decide if these statements are true (T) or false (F). Correct the false ones.**

	T	F
1) IMO means Insurance Maritime Organisation.	☐	☐
2) IMO is a European organisation.	☐	☐
3) It deals with pollution issues.	☐	☐
4) Construction standards are not among IMO's tasks.	☐	☐

14 Listen to an expert talking about safety in warehouses and complete the text with the missing words and expressions.

Most people do not know that the (1) _____ injury rate for the warehousing industry is (2) _____ than the average rate for industries in general. This may seem surprising but moving (3) _____ and materials can be a dangerous job! There are numerous potential (4) _____ in warehouses including unsafe use of forklift trucks, improper handling of materials, ergonomic hazards and slipping, tripping and (5) _____. To reduce the risk of accidents it is essential that potential hazards are communicated effectively to (6) _____ by employers. This may be done in the form of training courses, manuals and signs and (7) _____ in the workplace. Many warehouse activities also require the use of safety equipment, which must also be provided by the employer. These may include safety (8) _____, respiratory protection, (9) _____ and special overalls. Electrical systems are particularly sensitive and should always come with instructions for use, (10) _____ and emergency procedures. In case of emergency it is especially important that (11) _____ are clear and accessible and clearly marked, and that (12) _____ extinguishers are available and in good working order.

15 Complete the table referring to the text above.

Possible dangers	Safety measures
unsafe use of forklift trucks	*to communicate potential hazards*

Writing

16 Use the information from the text above to write a simple description explaining the meanings of the following signs used in the workplace.

_____

_____

_____

_____

Speaking

17 Which of the safety signs in this unit can you find in your school? Are there any other similar signs or warnings? Can you describe them and their meanings?

18 Prepare a short oral presentation giving your opinion on the importance of road safety. Use the information from the texts in this unit and the expressions below for help.

I think that... / In my opinion...

I'm for/against fleet monitoring... because...

Technical Terms

Employers' Liability (Compulsory Insurance) Act 1969　《1969雇主责任（强制保险）法》

Health and Safety (First Aid) Regulations 1981　《1981健康与安全（急救）条例》

Health and Safety Information for Employees Regulations 1989　《1989员工健康与安全信息条例》

Workplace Regulations 1992　《1992工作场所条例》

Personal Protective Equipment at Work Regulations 1992　《1992工作时个人防护设备条例》

Reporting of Injuries, Diseases and Dangerous Occurrences Regulations 1995 (RIDDOR)　《1995伤害、疾病与危险发生上报条例》

Provision and Use of Work Equipment Regulations 1998　《1998工作设备的提供与使用条例》

Management of Health and Safety at Work Regulations 1999　《1999工作健康与安全管理条例》

Control of Substances Hazardous to Health Regulations 2002 (COSHH)　《2002有害健康物质管制条例》

ABS (Anti-lock Braking System)　　　　　　　防抱死制动系统

Railway Safety Regulations　　　　　　　　　《铁路安全管理条例》

European Maritime Safety Agency (EMSA)　　　欧洲海事安全局

Learning Objectives

Upon completion of the unit, students will be able to:

- know how to write a CV and highlight personal strengths in it;
- master the words and expressions related to CV and interview;
- grasp proper skills to plan, prepare and succeed in an interview.

Starting Off

1 Work in pairs. Tick (√) the things you would expect to see in a CV and discuss why with your partner.

- [ ] address
- [ ] career history
- [ ] date of birth
- [ ] favourite TV programmes

- [ ] interests
- [ ] marital status
- [ ] name
- [ ] nickname

- [ ] qualifications
- [ ] social media presence

Reading 1

How to write a CV

A **curriculum vitae**, CV for short, is a brief **summary** of facts about you and your **qualifications**, **work history**, skills and experience. It is essential to have a good CV when **applying for** a job as it is your chance to sell yourself and be selected for an **interview**. Some companies may ask you to fill in an **application form** instead of sending a CV.

Your CV should be:

- **printed on white paper and no more than 2 or 3 **sides**;
- clear and correct;
- **positive** and make a good **impression**, **emphasising** your strengths and successes;
- **adapted to suit** the specific job profile.

Key features

Personal details
Your name, address, phone number(s), email address and date of birth.

Personal **profile**
This is normally at the beginning of the CV. It is a short statement aimed at selling yourself so you should use positive words and expressions. It must be **specifically** written for the **position** you are applying for.

Work experience

It is normal practice to list your most recent job first, with the dates. It is not a good idea to leave any gaps between dates and if you do not have a lot of experience, you should include details of part-time and **voluntary** work.

Qualifications and training

This includes qualifications from school and university as well as any other training courses or **certificates**. You should indicate the date (the most recent first), the title of the qualification, the level obtained and the organisation/place.

Achievements/skills/competences

This can include foreign languages and computer skills, as well as things like **artistic** or musical skills. It is possible to **highlight** a particular achievement — personal or professional — which **reflects** well on your ability to do the job.

Interests

Hobbies or sports activities can help show particular abilities or skills which could be **relevant** for the job.

References

This section is for the name, position and **contact details** of at least two people who can provide a personal and/or work reference. **Alternatively** it is possible to state that references can be supplied on request.

MY GLOSSARY

curriculum vitae (CV)		简历, 履历		specifically	adv.	明确地; 具体地
summary	n.	总结, 小结		position	n.	职位, 位置
qualification	n.	资格, 资历		voluntary	adj.	自愿的; 志愿的
work history		工作经历		certificate	n.	证书; 证明
apply for		应聘, 申请		achievement	n.	成绩, 成就
interview	n.	面试, 面谈		competence	n.	能力, 才干
application form		申请表		artistic	adj.	艺术的, 美术的
side	n.	（纸的）一面		highlight	v.	突出, 强调
positive	adj.	积极的; 建设性的		reflect	v.	反映; 显示
impression	n.	印象		relevant	adj.	相关的, 有关的
emphasise	v.	强调, 加强		reference	n.	推荐信, 介绍信
adapt to		适应; 改编		contact detail		联系方式
suit	v.	适合; 对……方便		alternatively	adv.	或者, 要不
profile	n.	简介, 概述				

2 Read the text and discuss these questions.

1) What is the purpose of a CV?

2) How long should it be? Why do you think that is?

3) Is it a good idea to use the same CV for different job applications? Why / Why not?

4) Why do you think the personal profile is normally at the start of the CV?

5) What order should you list your qualifications and previous jobs? Why do you think that is?

6) What kind of interests do you think would be positive to include in your CV? And negative?

7) What is the purpose of indicating references?

8) Can you think of other examples of positive words and expressions for a CV?

Reading 2

How to write a covering letter

Here you should refer to the **advertisement** and where you saw it. Include the **title** of the position and any reference number.

Here you can give a few details about your qualifications and/or experience.

This is your chance to state why you would be perfect for the company. Do not just use the same letter for every job application. Each letter should be **tailored** to the specific **requisites** mentioned in the ad.

Here you can mention any **enclosures** (CV, references, certificates) and state how you are going to follow up on your letter.

Colin Smith
7 High Street
Rochford
SS4 7PT
Tel: 01702 986631
colin.smith@virgin.net
17th April, 2020

Ms Zelda Gatsby,
Kraftyn Air,
83 Wimbledon Park Side, London
SW19 5LP

Dear Ms Gatsby,

I am writing in **response** to your advertisement in *The Guardian* and wish to apply for the **post** of Senior Shift Manager.

Since **graduating** with a first class degree in Business Administration in **Luton**, then after my degree in Engeneering from **Manchester** University, I have been working as a Manager in Logistics, first at XStandard Logistics in **Berlin** then at DeanAir Service Inc. UK. During both experiences, I have gained an excellent understanding of Logistics and Operations.

I have always enjoyed new **challenges** and of course working as a part of a team and I am confident that my experience of working in **extreme** conditions will enable me to face the demands that the position **entails**.

Please find **enclosed** my Curriculum Vitae and I would welcome the opportunity to provide further information during an interview.

I look forward to hearing from you.

Yours sincerely,

Colin Smith

Colin Smith

Enc.

advertisement	*n.*	广告, 宣传
title	*n.*	职位名称; 职称
tailor	*v.*	专门制作, 使适应特定需要
requisite	*n.*	必要条件; 必需品
enclosure	*n.*	（信中）附件
response	*n.*	回应, 回复
post	*n.*	职位;（尤指）要职

graduate	*v.*	毕业
Luton	*n.*	卢顿（英国城市）
Manchester	*n.*	曼彻斯特（英国城市）
Berlin	*n.*	柏林（德国首都）
challenge	*n.*	挑战, 考验
extreme	*adj.*	极端的; 极糟的
entail	*v.*	需要; 牵涉
enclose	*v.*	随函附上

3 Read the text and answer these questions.

1) Why is a covering letter important?

2) What two kinds of covering letter are there?

3) How should a covering letter be written?

4) How does a covering letter usually start?

5) Should a covering letter repeat all the details of a CV? Why / Why not?

6) Why is it not a good idea to use a standard covering letter for all applications?

Reading **3**

Tips for a successful interview

4 Think of four tips for a successful interview and discuss them with your partner. Then, read the article below. Are they the same with what you think of?

Job interviews can be stressful; however, with the proper planning and preparation, you can get the job. Read these tips to help you survive the interview and get the **job offer**.

Before the interview

- Reaserch the company and prepare relevant questions. **Interviewers** appreciate when job **candidates** show interest in the company and **available** position.
- Organise all **paperworks**, including your CV and eventual references from previous employers.
- Plan responses to common interview questions and practise interviewing with a **peer**.

- Prepare for questions about salary expectations by finding out how much employees in the position you are applying for are **typically** paid.

During the interview

- Make a good first impression by arriving on time for the interview. Make sure to dress in clean and professional **attire**. Finally, be polite and use the interviewer's name when speaking.
- **Respond** to all questions clearly. **Interviewees** should provide **solid** examples of how their previous experience relates to skills needed for the new position. Also be sure to explain your future career **goals**.

After the interview

- Employers may request a **call-back** to obtain more information as a **follow-up**.

MY GLOSSARY

job offer		工作机会	attire	n.	（尤指特定样式或正式的）服装, 衣着
interviewer	n.	面试考官, 主持面试者; 采访者			
candidate	n.	（竞选或求职的）候选人, 申请人	respond	v.	回答, 回应
			interviewee	n.	参加面试者; 接受采访者
available	adj.	可获得的; 可用的	solid	adj.	可靠的, 可信赖的
paperwork	n.	文件; 文书工作	goal	n.	目标, 目的
peer	n.	同龄人, 同辈	call-back	n.	回电
typically	adv.	通常, 一般	follow-up	n.	后续（行动）

5 Read the text and decide if these sentences are true (*T*) or false (*F*).

	T	F
1) A job candidate should ask about the company during the interview.	☐	☐
2) Interviewees make a good impression by dressing professionally for the interview.	☐	☐
3) A call-back is a typical way for a job candidate to follow up after an interview.	☐	☐
4) Talking about career goals and salary is not recommended.	☐	☐
5) You'd better provide CV and references upon request.	☐	☐
6) Before the interview, find out most of information about the company via web.	☐	☐

6 **Think of a company you would like to work for and write a covering letter. Use these points for your help:**

- You saw the advertisement on *The Guardian*;
- You looked at a logistic professionals website;
- You are interested to the open position of Air Export Gateway Manager;
- You will be in London in two weeks so would be available for an interview;
- You can currently speak English and Chinese;
- You gained 3 years' experience in the same role;
- You are available in 3 months starting from today.

7 **Write a dialogue with your partner simulating an interview according the CV below. Think about what to say, how to dress and what questions to ask and answer before the interview. After the interview, call your partner on the phone and tell him/her everything went well and thank him/her for being helpful.**

Example of a CV

Colin Smith
shift manager, logistics

Address	7 High Street, Rochford, SS4 7PT
Phone	01702 986631
Email	colin.smith@virgin.net

Personal profile

I am highly **motivated** and work well as part of a team. My professional experience at DeanAir Service Inc. as a Shift Manager taught me to adapt to new situations and to work under challenging conditions and high standard levels. I am now looking for a **senior** position to develop my career and duties.

Qualifications

2009 – 2012

Degree in **Engeneering**, Operations, Six Sigma Certified
Manchester University

2006 – 2008

Class **BS** degree in **Business Administration concentration** in Operations, Air Freight and German

Work history

November 2012

Shift Manager at DeanAir Service Inc., London

Sept. 2008 – June 2009

Assistant Manager at XStandard Logistics, Berlin

Interests

I enjoy chess, cycling and online videogame

References

Mr Günter Gratz
Shift Manager of XStandard Logistics
Berlin

Ms Susan Knight
General Manager DeanAir Service Inc.,
London

MY GLOSSARY

shift manager		值班经理	BS (Bachelor of Science)		理学学士	
motivate	v.	激励, 激发……的积极性	business administration		工商管理	
senior	adj.	级别高的	concentration	n.	专注, 集中	
engineering	n.	工程设计; 工程学	assistant manager		助理经理	

Speaking

8 Look at the CV in Exercise 7 and say whether it follows all the advice given in Reading 1.

9 Now discuss the suitability of the candidate for the job advertised.

Logistics Job Post - *The Guardian*

Senior Shift Manager
About the Job

- Our air freight company based in Heathrow requires the services of an experienced Shift Manager who can assume the management role for one of our more advanced teams working on a rotating schedule that changes each month. The successful applicant will be responsible for developing efficient work methods, and collaborating with employees to increase productivity while maintaining our strong safety record.
- Six Sigma and Engeneering Degree required, +5 years Shift Manager or Logistics preferred. If you have experience leading a team in the industry, please get in touch with us sending CV and covering letter to zeldagatsby@kraftynair.com

Job Summary

Company
Kraftyn Air, London

Location
London, UK

Job Type
- Full Time

1) What position is being advertised?

2) What requisites are they looking for?

3) Does the candidate have the right experience? And qualifications?

4) Does the CV make a positive impression? Why / Why not?

Technical Terms

Six Sigma Certificate　　六西格玛证书（一种技术资质证明）